The
Qabalah
of
50
Gates

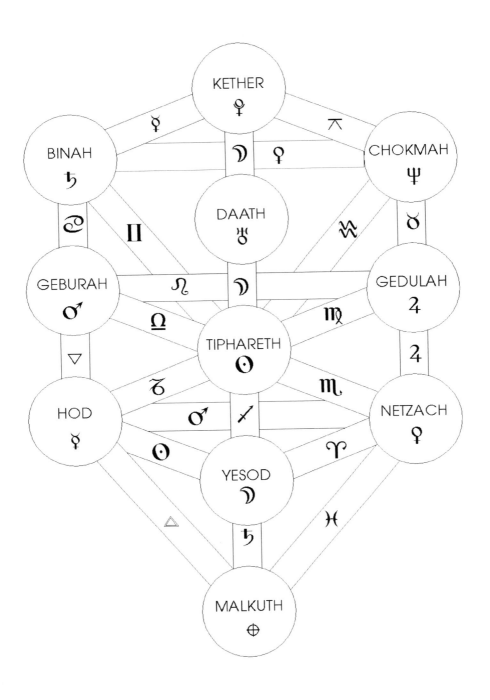

The Qabalah of 50 Gates

by
Steven Ashe

Mandrake

Published by
Mandrake of Oxford
PO Box 250
OXFORD
OX1 1AP (UK)

A CIP catalogue record for this book is available from the British Library and the US Library of Congress.

ISBN 1 869928 237

Printed & bound by Antony Rowe Ltd, Eastbourne

This work is for Robin Halverson
with much love

I would like to thank the following individuals for their help and encouragement with the manuscript, putting up with my close focus on the manuscript for many months and for making life enjoyable generally: Alex Ashe, David Ashe, Kestrel Isis Ashe, Martine Ashe, Rowan Ashe, Steven Ball, Paul Bolton, Ron Bonds of Illuminet Press U.S.A., Lawrence Brightman, Alex Bennett, Joan Corbett, Rick Cronan, Billy Ann Gargett, Shaun Goodwin, David Green, Liz Harnett, Steven Harrington, Ben Hassell, Bill Heidrick, John Hislop, Carolyn Hucker, Ket Keyte, Rick Keyte, Joanne Latham, Aine Lynch, MC Medusa, Mogg Morgan, Oz (Mahindra), Oxford Golden Dawn Occult Society, Brian Radley, Jason Smith, William Smith, Michael Staley, Robert and Patricia Turner, Laura Woodward, Donna Wright and all contributors to the alt.tarot newsgroup.

"I lived with them on Montague Street
In a basement down the stairs,
There was music in the cafes at night
And revolution in the air."

Bob Dylan

Steven Ashe was born in 1960 and has B.A. (Hons) Degree in Interactive Multimedia Communication. Prior to writing The Qabalah of 50 Gates his published work includes lectures delivered for The Oxford Thelemic Symposium (1994, 1995), production and voice-over credits for Aleister Crowley's The Book of the Law (Talking Book/Cassette – Illuminet Press, USA) and articles published in Prediction Magazine (May 1982) and the audio format Isis Magazine (1988). His interests include Cognitive Psychology, Humour, Acoustic Guitars and the history and design of Tarot Card iconography.

Contents

"I am knowing, and yet rarely known." The Goddess said to Kif in his dream. "If you would know me, you must sit in the deepest well in the city for three nights at the dark of the Moon." So Kif purchased an oversize bucket and had himself lowered into the well the next day.

The people of the town were amazed and a large crowd gathered around to witness his vigil. For three days and nights Kif remained in the well. To his surprise he found that he could see the stars of the heavens in the day time as well as at night. And so he became dumbstruck with awe.

When he was hauled up, Kif was summoned to the tent of the Caliph, who wished to learn what Kif had experienced down the well, and offered a meal and wine.

Refusing these, Kif requested a simple bowl of dates and a glass of goats milk which he consumed with relish. He was then brought before the Caliph who asked him: "What did the Goddess reveal of Herself to you, my son?"

Kif stared at him for a moment before replying. "In seeking the light, we are all blinded by it." He said. "It is what is beyond the light that should concern us: for the light shines out of a darkness which cradles us continuously.

"The Light is the Way, but the darkness is the beginning and the end."

"And how may we know the Goddess? How is it that we may come to know the unknowable?" The Caliph further pursued.

"By living simple lives." Kif replied. "And by learning that one must descend into the darkness in order to see beyond the light."
The Nineteenth Gate (Kether of Yesod)

Preface

Mogg Morgan

It gives me great pleasure to try to introduce the work of an old wanderer in Kabbalistic 'wasteland' – Brother Steven Ashe. This is not an introductory kabbalistic text – goodness knows there are enough of them in circulation – several of which are mentioned below. What follows is an initiate's journey through a particularly obscure and largely unexplored territory; told in the form of a fictional narrative. Well I suggest you cut to the chase now and start enjoying this latter day pilgrim's progress from life to the 'City of the Pyramids'. But for the perplexed I offer a few more words by way of my own personal prolegomena to Steven's eloquent parables and meditations.

Whatever the literal meaning of the word 'Kabbalah'[1] it actually denotes the magical tradition within Judaism. For various reasons this secret tradition has exerted a huge influence on Hermetic or Western magick for at least the last 500 years. Since, that is, the expulsion of the Jews from Spain in 1492 by the authoritarian Christian monarchs Ferdinand and Isabella. The upshot of the destruction of Jewish centres of learning was the spread of Kabbalistic ideas throughout Europe and the publication of ideas that previously had only been transmitted by word of mouth. Many Kabbalistic ideas are very ancient and formulated in the last few centuries before the dawn of the common era.[2] These important magical ideas were formed in the melting pot which included

Greek magic, gnosticism and concepts from Egypt, Persian and even India.

The Magical Journey

One of the most important ideas of the Kabbalah is the inner magical journey, accomplished through a complex series of ritual techniques. If successful the magician sees god face to face. Thereby the magician obtains the complete knowledge of the 'torah' or law. But unlike the boring academic knowledge of the priest, the magician has a direct and mystical understanding of the real laws that govern the universe. Kabbalists use a variety of mystical diagrammes as useful tools in their spiritual journeying. The most famous of these is the Tree of Life (see diagram). In its modern form this is a model of ten or eleven spheres joined by twenty-two pathways. The model as a 'means of knowledge' is often underestimated in western thought but is a mystery worthy of meditation in itself. The Kabbalistic Tree of Life model, as well as several lesser know Kabbalistic diagrams have been extremely important to present day magical culture.

Other aspects of Kabbalah

Some magicians use the Kabbalah as a kind of magical model, a way of mapping out the inner landscape and also a journey of initiation. Many magical systems start with elemental rituals - obtaining knowledge and experience of the four elements. This initiation can be seen as the initiation of Malkuth, the 'lowest' sphere on the tree of life, with which the four elements are traditionally associated.

There are 'virtues' and 'vices' typically linked to each sphere; for Malkuth the 'vice' is said to be inertia, and it is this inertia that serious magicians must overcome if they are to pursue the Great Work.

Another practice associated with Malkuth is the creation of an 'astral temple' which the magician visits in the course of a visualisation, and which contains certain ritual objects like the double cube altar, one black and one white cube, and where you may meet Sandalphon, the Archangel of the sphere. Useful in itself as practice in strengthening your powers of visualisation, astral contact with Sandalphon may give information about the nature of things.

Later you might move on to Yesod, which is ruled by the moon (the seven spheres above Malkuth on the glyph are associated with the seven traditional planets) and is typically the realm of illusions, and the development of psychic abilities; or Netzach, when many magicians perform the practice 'Liber Astarte', described in Crowley's Magick in Theory and Practice, which involves developing devotion to one particular deity. The initiation of Tiphareth, to give another example, is associated with the 'Knowledge and Conversation of the Holy Guardian Angel', that is the re-integration with your 'higher Self'. More information can be found in Dion Fortune's The Mystical Qabalah - but be prepared to take some of her pronouncements, especially about 'racial dharmas' with several pinches of salt.

The Pentagram rite

Even magicians who rarely study the Kabbalah in detail often employ Kabbalistic symbolism when they perform the classic banishing ritual - the pentagram rite. This rite involves the 'kabbalistic cross', which involves the visualision of the tree of life within your own body.

To do this, first imagine yourself growing larger and larger, your body expanding, until your head is among the stars and your feet thousands of miles below on the earth.

Directly above your head imagine a ball of pure white light of fantastic effulgence. Feel it glowing at the crown of your head, and touch your forehead and vibrate (chant or hum so that it resonates) 'Ator' (meaning 'thou art').

Then imagine the light shooting down through your body and forming another ball at your feet, way, way beneath you. Touch your abdomen and vibrate 'Malkuth' (the Kingdom).

Then, imagine another white ball of light at your left shoulder, as bright as before, and vibrate 've Geburah' (the power), which then sweeps across to your right shoulder as you chant 've Gedulah' (and the glory).

Finally, keeping clearly in your mind the sensation of the cross of dazzling white light pulsating through your body, clasp your hands at the centre of the cross over your heart and vibrate 'le olam' (to the world), 'Amen'.

In this rite you are drawing down the force of Kether, ('crown') the top sphere on the glyph, through your body, and visualizing, and sensing the entirety of the tree of life within you. It is a pity that magicians sometimes rush this exercise and go on to perform the rest of the pentagram rite without dwelling a little longer on this beginning. Israel Regardie's book The Middle Pillar is a useful introduction to this, and develops further the ideas described here.

The First Kabbalist

The first Kabbalist was Enoch, who is mentioned only briefly in the book of Genesis (5.21) as the son of Cain, who 'walked with god. Kabbalistically - Enoch saw god and did not ever die. He accomplished the highest magical attainment and virtually became a god. In mythology he is said to share ancestry with Noah going back to Seth, the third son of Adam born after the death of Abel. He is one of the mythical heroes that roamed the world before the catastrophe of the flood. He lived for 365 years, which is the writer's way of telling us that he has connection with the sun god and was initiated into the mysteries of earth and heaven and all its divine secrets. (In Peake's commentary he says that Enoch may be identical with Emmeduranki, the King of Sippar, in Mesopotamia, a favourite of the gods, (especially the sun-god). The Third book of Enoch[3] is of paramount importance for practicing magicians. It tells us how Enoch became Metatron, the greatest of all the Kabbalistic angels second only in importance to the God himself. Written about 2000 years ago, it is likely that the practice can be traced back even further to places like ancient Egypt. The legends of Enoch show that the ancient Hebrews didn't just believe in one god. In Enoch's book of secrets he wrote famously of seven palaces or heavens and this is the older way of representing the cabbalistic journey, not as a lineal tree but as a circle. The two lower spheres (Malkuth and Yesod) are treated as one sphere, and the three upper spheres (Kether, Binar and Hokmah) are combined as one, the whole makes a neat arrangement of six stages encircling the sun in the centre (see diagram). Enoch describes in great detail his long journey through the seven different heavens - in the second we find the abode of the fallen angels, in the third the seat of paradise and in the seventh the throne of god himself. The name Enoch constantly recurs within the magical tradition. The Elizabethan Magus John Dee obtained a new magical language and system called Enochian by direct communication with discarnate angelic beings.

This very same trance journey technique was probably the one that passed into the tradition of the early Celtic Church who called it Aisling. Early Celtic churches are small, intimate buildings very suitable for mystical meditation and journeying. With the coming of the Norman church, this whole tradition was suppressed (See Myles Dillon and Nora Chadwick *Celtic Realms*) Here's a little example based upon Z'ev *Rhythmajik*:

After the usual preparation, we played a little ambient music and visualised a green curtain. We passed through this into a verdant natural landscape. We moved up a regular hill to see a long barrow at the summit. Looking over this we imagined that it was divided by chalk grooves, marking out nine regular segments (like the board for noughts and crosses). These we explored in our own time but taking note of the number and position of any entities or experiences encountered along the way. For example I saw lots of images in the first, the fifth and the seventh chambers.

Another important figure in the development of Kabbalistic magical ideas must be the Old Testament prophet Ezekiah. Read his book afresh forgetting all the rubbish laid on this by the Christians. Ezekiah lived in hard times and at the time he wrote many of his prophecies had actually happened. Through mortification and magical practice he obtained an apocalyptic vision of god, who came down to earth in a fiery chariot (Merkavah in Hebrew). This gives its name to this whole school of magical Kabbalah.

Testing Visions

The problem that confronts any magician working in this kind of area is, having obtained important visions, how do you test their veracity? Below are some commonly used techniques, so common that many think it is all there is to Kabbalah. Thus one reads statements about Kabbalah being a 'cosmic filing system' etc., which make Kabbalah look very boring indeed. I repeat, Kabbalah is a complete system of magick.

A large part of Kabbalistic trance work involves discussion and meditation of symbols and words. For some mystics this is a means (although not the only means) of trance induction in itself. The Greek philosopher Socrates could also 'think' himself into a trance. He often emerged from these states possessed by real knowledge. Kabbalists traditionally use three methods of mystical analysis - Gematria, Notariqon, and Temura.

Gematria is a form of numerology that stems from fact that Hebrew and Greek do not have any numerals. Counting is done using the same characters also used for spelling. Thus A = 1, B = 2 etc. A full list of these is shown in any Hebrew dictionary or in roman characters only at the end of this fact-sheet. Thus any word is also a number. But because this number is not immediately obvious, Gematria is often used to look for secret keys or equivalence's between words obtained in a vision. One of the earliest examples of Gematria is found in the Old Testament. Abram and his wife Sarai, managed to produce an heir after many years of barrenness. Their names immediately change from Abram to Abraham, and Sarai to Sarah. Numerically Sarai name has decreased by five and Abraham has increased by five. This symbolises the gift of a baby by Sarah to Abraham.

Notariqon means shorthand and is the practice of summarising an important magical formula in terms of a single word. For example VITRIOL from the tarot card ART, which stands for Visita Interiora Terra Rectificando Invenies Occultum Lapidem - 'Visit the interior parts of the earth by rectification thou shalt find the hidden stone.'[4]

Temura means permutation, or a kind of code using the Kabbalistic system, the most important form is known as the Kabbalah of Nine Chambers which groups letters of the Hebrew alphabet in chambers according to their arithmetical powers. For example the first chamber is: Shin = 300, Lamed = 30, Gimel = 3

All nine chambers look so:

300	30	3	200	20	2	100	10	1
Sh(ש)	L(ל)	G(ג)	R(ר)	K(כ)	B(ב)	Q(ק)	I(י)	A(א)
600	60	6	500	50	5	400	40	4
M*(ם)	S(ס)	V(ו)	K*(ך)	N(נ)	H(ה)	Th(ת)	M(מ)	D(ד)
900	90	9	800	80	8	700	70	7
Tz*(ץ)	Tz(צ)	T(ט)	P*(ף)	P(פ)	Ch(ח)	N*(ן)	O(ע)	Z(ז)

* Some Hebrew letter have a special form when they occur at the end of a word, the so called 'final form'
A code can be made from this in which ù represents those letters that

lie in the central chamber, i.e. K *, N or H. 'Codes' like this can be useful for generating information.

The Kabbalah of 50 Gates, seems to combine elements of all the above. But I was reminded most of the ideas in Joseph Campbell's 'Hero With A Thousand Faces'. Campbell recalls a Hebrew version of the Kabbalah's creation: Cabalistic texts such as the Zohar (light, splendor) are collections of esoteric Hebrew writing given to the world in about 1305 by a learned Spanish Jew, Moses de Leon. It was claimed that such material had been drawn from secret originals, going back to the teachings of Simeon ben Yohai, a rabbi of Galilee in the second century AD. Threatened with death by the Romans, Simeon had hidden for twelve years in a cave; ten centuries later his writings had been found there and these were the sources used by the author of the Zohar.

Simeon's teachings were supposed to have been drawn from the *hokmah nistarah* or hidden wisdom of Moses, i.e. a body of esoteric lore first studied by Moses in Egypt, the land of his birth, then pondered by him during his forty years in the wilderness (where he received special instruction from an angel), and finally incorporated cryptically in the first four books of the Bible, from which it can be extracted by a proper understanding and manipulation of the mystical number-values of the Hebrew alphabet. This lore and the techniques for rediscovering and utilizing it constitute the cabala.

It is said that the teachings of the cabala ('received or traditional lore') were first entrusted by God himself to a special group of angels in Paradise. After Man had been expelled from the garden, some of these angels communicated the lessons to Adam, thinking to help him back to felicity thereby. From Adam the teaching passed to Noah, and from Noah to Abraham. Abraham let some of it slip from him while he was in Egypt, and that is why this sublime wisdom can now be found in reduced form in the myths and philosophies of the gentiles. Moses first studied it with the priests of Egypt, but the tradition was refreshed in him by the special instruction of his angels. (p. 267-8)

In the Hero with a Thousand Faces, Joseph Campbell talks about a thing he calls the monomyth. The monomyth is a myth that can be identified in the stories and legends of most of the world cultures, almost like the collective story of humanities spiritual path. Elements of the monomyth can be found in ancient Greek or Egyptian myth or even in modern sagas like the film Star Wars. A earlier mythography, J G Frazer, tried in his monumental study The Golden Bough, to do a similar thing, although his work is a lot largely superseded now by that of Joseph Campbell. I have found it interesting the compare Joseph Campbell's monomyth with the evolutionary schema of the cabablistic tree of life. The monomyth is a kind of spiritual, sometimes physical journey. It can be broken down into three phases:

Departure - Initiation – Return

1.   The Departure phase can in turn be broken down into several steps, although in myth these steps may be mixed up. The steps are

i. Call to adventure
ii. Refusal of the Call
iii. Supernatural Aid
iv. Crossing the first threshold

v. Failure, obstruction and delay, what Campbell compare to Jonah's capture in the Belly of the Whale. All of these stages seem to me to have something in common with the lower spheres on the tree of Life, especially Malkuth (the Earth) and Yesod (realm of water/moon/ illusion etc).

2.   Initiation is probably a continuous process but includes, according to Campbell the following steps:

i.   Road of Trials

ii.   Meeting With the Goddess.
iii.   Woman as temptress
iv.   Atonement with the Father
v.   Apotheosis
vi.   Ultimate Reward. Again these can be matched up with many of the experiences of the central portion of the Tree of Life.

3. The Path of Return is more difficult to place, does I return by the way I came or can this be likened to the crossing of the higher abyss in the Tree of life and the integration of the realm of the gods and that of the material world? Joseph Campbell talks of the following steps:

i.   Refusal of the Return
ii.   Magical Flight or Chase (as in Jason's return with the Golden Fleece)
iii.   Rescue from without
iv.   Crossing the return threshold
v.   Master of two worlds
vi.   vi. Freedom to live.

This journey aspect is a key part of contemporary magical practice and the use of imaginal or astral journeying is a fairly common group and individual technique. It goes back at least as far as the third (and most magical) Book of Enoch mentioned above. Well that's enough of my ramblings in hyper reality. I'm just trying to wet your appetite for a novel and more romantic approach to the ancient magical tradition of the Kabbalah and the mysteries of its fifty gates.

Further Research
Kabbalah is a big subject and I have only scraped the surface. To proceed further you need to do some reading and research of your own. As a suggestion for further reading you could do worse than the

Kabbalah FAQ available, if you have a computer, via the Internet.

Notes
1. Tradition, perhaps secret or oral variety
2. Sometimes termed BC
3. This book is difficult to obtain but if there is sufficient interest Mandrake may undertake a reprint.
4. Crowley, *Book of Thoth*

General Introduction to the Qabalah

QBL, or Qabalah, is a word signifying a verbal tradition or secret religious lore, and translates literally from the Hebrew as 'from mouth to ear'.

According to the Qabalistic tradition, God created the Universal Schema through spoken utterances and commands.

The Ten Spheres upon the Tree of Life glyph are the divine Sephiroth [more properly 'Sephiroth Belimah' - 'Voices from Nothing'] which symbolically represent the Decad of Creation.

The decimal unit was taken by the originators of the Qabalah, who saw in the number ten a measure of perfection, to represent the trinity of the god-head working through the Seven Days of Creation. The Hebrew letters Yod, Heh and Vau are the letters of the name IHVH which compose this pre-Christian trinity.

The number three has always been linked to the concept of the god-head, mainly due to its links to the concept of Eternity. The Creators three-fold aspect is 'He that has always existed', 'He that exists' and 'He that shall endure for ever'.

The idea of an infinite and immortal God, who reveals himself in a Universe he has fashioned from the substance of His own being represents a paradox. The Qabalist is human, and therefore limited by his own mortality. He therefore finds himself having to deal with the problem of having to relate to an immortal Creator dealing with his creation, and also the paradox of his own place in Eternity as a being limited within a four dimensional perceptual frame reference.

As a starting point, and even this may take several lifetimes to master, the Qabalah attempts to arrive at an understanding of one single aspect of the Creator through the study of numerology and meditation upon the sacred hieroglyphs of the Hebrew alphabet. Because the system of the Qabalah represents the esoteric side of the Judaic religious lore it contains many keys which unlock texts contained in the Old testament. In the Hebrew tongue, letters of the alphabet stand double duty as numbers. For example, the letter Aleph may also be written for the character representing number One.

Every word and phrase therefore has a numerological value.

The Hebrew phrase 'IHVH AChD' ["The Eternal reveals himself through unity"] adds to the number 39. There are Thirty Nine separate works in the Hebrew canonical works which comprise the Old Testament. Also, the number of Hebrew letters in the titles of the Ten Sephiroth total thirty nine in all. Thus can the Qabalistic significance of the phrase IHVH AChD be realised.

Other codes contained in the text of the Old Testament include a series of three verses which run concurrently in the Book of Exodus; each comprised of seventy two letters. These are Exodus 14: 19, 20 and 21.

If these verses are set out - each in a straight line reading from right to left in the normal Semitic practice, one above the other, with the middle verse [verse twenty] reversed so that it reads from left to right, then seventy two tri-lateral columns of angelic names are formed. According to Aleister Crowley in his "Book of Thoth", these names may be arrived at from the tri-syllable combinations in the same fashion that crossword solutions may be gleaned through paying attention to the known letters of the word you are seeking and filling in the blanks.

The above mentioned list of names constitute the hierarchy of powers known as the Angels of the Schemahamphorash [Divided Name"]. All of this will be studied by advanced Qabalists, but the beginner will have to begin from basics such as the Hebrew alphabet and the Sephiroth.

I would advise the newcomer to disregard the list of the Schemahamphorash to be found in Regardie's 'Golden Dawn' as this work contains elementary mistakes in the rendering of six of the angelic names obtained from the columns of Exodus 14, verses 19, 20 and 21.

The Qabalah: It's Origin & Development

The exact date of the origin of the esoteric system known as the Qabalah is a scholarly mystery. Ancient tradition recounts that the secret doctrine enshrined in Qabalistic lore was communicated directly to Adam by the Archangel Ratziel, who passed it on to successive generation by word of mouth. By a similar method the Qabalah has survived the millennia and has only in recent times been committed to writing in a somewhat incomplete format - for it has always been an oral tradition surviving exclusively in the Rabbinical caste.

Whatever the true origins of Qabalistic philosophy, its original foundations are certainly contemporary with Jehovah [IHVH] worship amongst the Semitic peoples. Certainly these foundations existed long enough before the Pentateuch [first five books of the Old Testament] for them to be incorporated into the essence of this collection of writings which was written circa 1500 BC [Era Vulgaris].

The canonical works of the Hebrew Testament are remarkable in that they are strictly exoteric in nature; dealing with worldly and materialistic philosophies, laws and codes of moral behaviour. The esoteric side of Judaism was, in the main, left open to the interpretation of qualified teachers [Rabbi's] whose meditations upon the 'letters of the law' incorporated Qabalistic doctrine in order to gain an understanding of the divine Cosmogony. In this way the Qabalah evolved, for now and then great teachers of penetrating insight would discern fresh and deeper insights into the lore. Each building upon the successes of those who had passed that way before him.

Wynn Westcott in "The Magical Mason" [Ed. R.A. Gilbert] notes the similarity in the development of the Qabalah alongside Old Testament sources to the relationship between the esoteric Upanishads of the Hindus and the more exoteric Brahmana texts.

In both cases the 'secret' knowledge was kept strictly apart from the profane texts as this knowledge was for the eyes of only the most worthy. For many centuries the Qabalistic doctrines continued to be passed on by word of mouth and doubtless varied and evolved by the minds through which it filtered.

The first Qabalistic work dealing with the Sephiroth and the letters of the Hebrew alphabet to be published was the Sepher Yetzirah - The Book of Formation which surfaced circa 22 A.D - composed of a synthesis of partially complete ancient versions. This work is a philosophical commentary upon the Creation - drawing a parallel between the works of creation [origin of the Earth, Sun, Planets, Elements, etc] - and the twenty two letters of the Hebrew alphabet and their combinations which the Source employed in the act of creation. To these twenty two letters are added the ten Sephiroth, thus revealing the Thirty two Paths of Wisdom.

The Sepher Yetzirah was strongly influenced by Judaic Merkabah mysticism which employed meditative techniques to induce trance vision and the apparent experience of astral projection.

Through Merkabah techniques the practitioner would rise through the planes in his astral form, where he would perceive the Almighty seated on his Throne or Chariot [Merkabah]. This journey would be perilous in the extreme for deadly beings were held to guard the gateways to the astral planes in order to prevent unworthy souls from spiritual ascent. Only the knowledge of the correct keys and the magical names of power could ensure the safe passage of the Soul during Merkabah projection: a philosophy borrowed by the later Gnostics, which underpins their beliefs in the souls confrontation of the Archons at the gates of the seven planes during the after-life.

Around 200 AD two distinct schools of Qabalistic thought had evolved. That is, the understanding of the idea of God arrived at by two separate areas of concentration - the study of the numbers [or Sephiroth] and the study of the 22 letters [the Schema].

The second Qabalistic treatise to be made public was the Sepher Zohar [the Book of Splendour], published circa 1290 AD by Rabbi Moses de Leon of Guadalajara, Spain. Like the Sepher Yetzirah, this work is a synthesis of separate treatises written by numerous Rabbis throughout the ages.

According to the lore of the tradition the literary back-bone of the Sepher Zohar was originally committed to writing by Rabbi Simeon ben Jochai, who completed this task around 160 AD after being driven into living in exile in a cave by Lucius Aurelius Verus the co-regent with the Roman Emperor Marcus Aurelius Antoninus.

By the time this work came to be published by Rabbi Moses de Leon it had been added to by other hands, and the main task of its editor lay in synthesising the extant literature into a coherent format. From this time onwards, the main body of Merkabah inspired Qabalistic doctrine fell into the domain of medieval magick and ceremonial occultism. Manuscript copies of the Sepher Zohar were in general circulation until three official codices of the work appeared in the late sixteenth and early seventeenth centuries. These were the Mantua codex of 1558, the Cremona Codex of 1590 and the Lublin codex of 1628 which were printed in the Hebrew language.

The philosophies imbedded in both the Sepher Yetzirah and the Zohar imply a belief in the hierarchical arrangement of the Universe of which Man is held to be a microcosm. This provided Qabalistic scholars with a ladder of mystical ascent which could be 'climbed' by anyone who correctly employed the time held magical Names of Power in their meditations upon the divine being.

The System of the Fifty Gates explored in the present work, when laid alongside the more traditionally accepted systems of 'pathworking', unites the mysteries of the numbers and the letters of the Sepher Yetzirah.

When the Fifty meet the Twenty Two, the Seventy Two angels of the Schemhamphorasch [held to be the leaves upon the Tree of Life] may be understood by the Wise.

The Rosicrucian 'Cabalah'

Another thread in the tapestry of arcane wisdom which many authorities fail to distinguish from the Qabalah is the founding of the Cabala - the Sufi oriented semantic system - which has influenced many prominent philosophers and teachers and which links into the history of the Spanish Qabalah.

This system may be thought of as being similar in nature to Zen in its teaching methods. It is rooted in the Language of the Birds [the 'green language' which has infiltrated the western alchemic tradition] and examples of the use of the methods of the 'Cabala' which writers upon the Qabalah have employed may be found in the works of Kenneth Grant and the French alchemist writing under the name of Fulcanelli.

The Arabic word WIRD, signifying the 'developmental exercise' practices of the Sufis has often been used by the Sufi mystical poets as WaRD, meaning Rose.

The Arabic root SLB, meaning to 'extract the marrow' was also often employed alongside the former as SLB WIRD, translating as "to obtain the core essence of the exercise". Another rendering of the root SLB also translates as 'Cross'.

According to Idries Shah writing in his 'History of the Sufi's', it is this misunderstanding of Arabic grammar that has confused those standing outside, and not infrequently inside, the Rosicrucian tradition.

And he has a case. It is certainly true that the Renaissance, and the ensuing Age of Enlightenment would not have been possible but for the spread of the Arab wisdom through Moorish Spain into Europe from the late eighth century onwards.

The Arabs had preserved the classics of the ancient world and the algebra of ancient India. After the Crusades precious works thought lost to western civilisation suddenly became available.

The Age of the Crusades was only cooling when the Renaissance flowered. Crusading in the Middle East against the infidel, and the internal European Crusades against such heresies as the Cathar/ Albigensian movement, had been launched to combat the expansion of the intellectual arena of the Islamic world. This latter, due mainly to the Moorish occupation of South Western Spain, had fostered an intellectual climate that made the popularisation and printing of the Sepher Zohar in the Thirteenth century possible.

The modern conception of the Rosicrucian Tradition, - the version favoured by such allegedly authoritative sources as the Victorian Golden Dawn - with it's tales of the travels of Christian Rosencranz seems childishly naive to any informed and disinterested onlooker. Even taken allegorically this mythos fails to satisfy, and appears shallow in the extreme.

Modern and supposedly authoritative books published upon the subject of Rosicrucianism and the hermetic Qabalah fail to raise the issue of a

Sufi heritage. Many of the authors, whilst fully aware of the existence of the groups of philosophers claimed over the ages as Rosicrucian initiates, seem unable or unwilling to provide supporting evidence for a 'strong theory' focus on the Arabian source of the concept of Rosicrucianism.

Both Johann Duns Scotus and his protégé Thomas Aquinas were reputed to be able to sight read the prophet in his native tongue. Ramon Lull, claimed by many 'authorities' as a true Rosicrucian and whose philosophical efforts brought us the 'Rosicrucian Qabalah' [or 'Spanish Qabalah'] was bi lingual in the Islamic vernacular - he was stoned to death in the Holy Land trying to convert the natives to Christianity.

In the spirit of the above, one other name stands out in the history of philosophy as a likely catalyst to the tradition that has come down to us as the rather anaemic, 'fake', 'Rosicrucianism' of the kind practiced by those uncritical enough to tow the 'Golden Dawn' line without question. That name is Michael Scott, the utopian thinker and Court Philosopher to Emperor Frederick II of Sicily - an island with a history of Moorish occupation and religious and architectural culture, where he no doubt came under the influence of schools of Sufi thought.

Scott had a public reputation for performing miracles that would put any self respecting wonder working Rabbi to shame, and is also reported to have been adept at inducing visions by a combination of manipulation of light and suggestion; a phenomenon strongly associated with Sufi adepts. It is possible that his familiarity with, and translation of, the texts of Arabian medicine and philosophy inspired much speculation upon his alleged alchemical prowess, and also concerning his later influence upon tales alluded to in later Rosicrucian texts. He was even mentioned by Dante - himself a student of the Spanish Saracen derived language of Provence, the chosen idiom of the authors of the Troubadour Courtly Romances - in his Divine Comedy (Inferno, Canto XX, lines 115-117).

The later published allegorical tales of the Rosicrucians, especially the legends concerning events in the life of Christian Rosencranz, evidently had some foundation in the myths circulated amongst the common people of the Middle Ages concerning the teachings and adventures of the great philosophers of the era.

The Qabalah of Fifty Gates

The Qabalistic Tree of Life glyph is composed of ten Sephiroth, twenty two Paths [which are in effect the combined influences of the Sephiroth] and fifty Gates which constitute states of mind generated by our experience of the Sephiroth and the twenty two Paths.

The traditional Qabalistic interpretation of the 'Four Hundred Desirable Worlds' is challenged by the model of the Tree of Life implied by the Thelemic system of the Fifty gates. In the traditional system, a microcosmic blueprint of the ten Sephiroth is contained in each individual Sephirah throughout each of the Four Qabalistic Worlds - yielding Four Hundred possible worlds.

In the system of the Fifty Gates, each Sephirah of the Tree is thought to contain only the blueprint of the Sephiroth preceding it upon the Tree plus the potentia of it's own mystical experience.

Chesed, the fourth Sephirah, is therefore thought to contain the 'genetic blueprint' of Kether, Chokmah and Binah - which precede it - plus the potentia of the divine force of Love; it's own qualitative experience: four gates in all.

Using this new system, fifty such gates separate the noumenal world of the lowest gate in Malkuth, from the Supernal Triad of Kether, Chokmah, Binah. Daath, the void created by Malkuth during 'The Fall' alluded to in Genesis representing the Fiftieth of the Gates.

The system of the Qabalah of Fifty Gates may initially perhaps best be approached as an organised exploration of the psychological 'mindsets' and webs of psycho-sexual dynamics which underlie our belief systems - the raggle taggle amalgams of working hypotheses which colour our outlook upon the world we interface with day by day.

As one advances through the gates, sometimes "in turn" at other times "at once", the aspirant will sublimate the prima-materia of the lower-ego personality and advance through the higher gates to confront psycho-spiritual and sexo-spiritual personal dynamics.

Next, techniques may be harnessed by Initiates working within the sphere of the 'mid heaven gates' to catapult the throne of the lower consciousness through the veil of Paroketh which clouds access to the experience of the Holy Guardian Angel in Tiphareth and the Cubic Stone of the Six Gates.

These technique of involves the blending of the aspirations of the personality towards immortality and the flow of the potential energies which vitalise the individuals drive towards survival. These 'higher' potential energies are considered by many modern initiates to be focused by the 'Over-Self' entity - portrayed by the metaphor of the Holy Guardian Angel after the publication of Samuel Liddell Mather's 'Magic of Abramelin the Mage' in the Golden Dawn tradition - from the realm of Eternity [the non dimensional realm of the Ain Soph, above the Tree of Life].

In a sense, this requires a blending of the subconscious and super-conscious [ego], subjectivity and objectivity. The Book of the Law states "There is division hither homewards": it is this 'division' that provides the catalyst for change and evolutionary development. Gurdjieff talked of a 'Third World' and a 'Third Force' lying between reality and perception; J.G. Bennett discusses 'Hazard'; Austin Osman Spare talks of an 'in-between' reality and Jan Fries of a 'Siedways'.

Similarly, the 50 Gates are purely experiential. Perception of their qualities is reliant upon the innate mental structures which underpin the individual's mental representations upon which his or her world view is constructed.

The experience of the Fifty Gates is similar to the art of pathworking, but momentary and hauntingly elusive. One steps into and through each of the Gates and receives a quanta of enlightenment akin to the spark burning in the lamp of the Hermit of the Tarot, which lights his surroundings.

Given that each of us is a Microcosm of a greater, but divided whole, we can only hope to know the Creator through the Creation: within the sphere of influence represented by Tiphareth upon the Tree of Life, composed of the six potentials of the gates of that matrix which marry the Macrocosm to the Microcosm.

According to the Neo-Platonic model of the Qabalah as evinced by Frances Yates, Man is regarded as a microcosm of the whole of the Creation. And the Creation itself, a mere microcosm of the Creator.

Even a microcosm of the Microcosm (a Nanocosm) may, according to the logic underlying the modus operandi of Qabalistic lore, contain the key to 'knowing' the Macrocosm. For the identity of the Macrocosm is held to reveal itself through the processes of Creation which have remained consistent since the first three minutes after the Big Bang event.

The system of the Fifty Gates provides a missing link between Qabalistic Magic and Mysticism for it posits the following: The processes involved in the creation of a Nanocosm in relation to a microcosm must be consistent with the process involved in the creation of a Microcosm in relation to a Macrocosm.

Therefore the Nanocosm may know the Macrocosm by observing it's interactive relationship with, and it's origins in the Microcosm.

'Working the Fifty Gates' is therefore a process of Self realisation and empowerment through guided visionary self-confrontation and self-observation requiring great impartiality of prejudice.

At the commencement, it is a system which attempts to help the aspirant identify the elements of his or her own psychological make-up which constitute the contact points between the Self and the Source. Contact points which may be 'worked on' and fine tuned in order to better 'walk the paths' between the Sephiroth.

Indeed, one must be intimately familiar with the virtues *and* vices of Sephiroth of the Qabalistic Tree in order to pass through the 50 Gates. But one must understand their significance as portals for transformation as, similarly, one must understand that the paths of the Tree are not always pathways that are mentally walked. More often, these paths represent states of being. In a similar way, the experiences of the 50 Gates represent processes of 'becoming'.

If my treatment of some of the experiences associated with the Qabalah of 50 gates appears sometimes flippant, then sometimes overly serious, be warned that this is deliberate.

In two instances I have reworked traditional Sufi parables to suit the instance, and I am indebted to Idries Shah for his rendering of these in his excellent work 'Caravan of Dreams'.

The Ten Astro-Physical Gates of Malkuth

The ten astro-physical gates of Malkuth all exist in the world of Assiah [the Qabalistic World of Action]. They are therefore all linked to the neural balance of the aspirant determined by the body's hormonal alchemy, and may be attitudinal, psycho-sexual or mood inspired.

The First Gate (Malkuth of Malkuth)

Physical Discipline and exertion to break the veil of inertia of the material and noumenal. Any ritual act performed in sincerity, having as its intent the harmonising of the 'astro-spiritual' with the 'astro-physical' will open this gate.

It is the state of mind associated with the Hexagram - the meeting of Macrocosm and Microcosm - generated by initiation through effort.

The Second Gate (Yesod of Malkuth)

The identification of the roots of your own sexual desire through self confrontational interfaces with reality, in the fact of the present moment or in the glamour of memory. The state of self awareness experienced by the lower ego personality peculiar to orgasm generated by sex-fantasy rites.

Twists in the purity of the next of the gates [Hod of Malkuth] may be detected in the strength by which the aspirant detects the nature of the sexual fantasy deviating from a 'norm' which can be reconciled with the 'conscience'.

The Third Gate (Hod of Malkuth)

The ideology of ruthlessness applied to self disciplined effort. This gate may be accessed by fasting and abstinence as it may be penetrated through exerting the effort of the lower will of the 'intellect-personality'. Where the desires are unharnessed and in a state of 'Will under Love' this gate remains closed resulting in the build-up of unfocussed emotional charges which have not been sublimated by behavioural processing.

The Fourth Gate (Netzach of Malkuth)

The ideology of surrender within the context of sexual union. This gate may be opened through sexual exhaustion and also through intoxication by "wine and strange drugs". The fourth gate's essence is the affirmation of the 'Will to survive' expressed through sexual activity.

The Fifth gate (Tiphareth of Malkuth)

The evolutionary aspiration expressed in the joy of orgasm and sexual bonding. This gate may be 'entered' through that state of mind generated by desire and sexual ambition.

The Sixth Gate (Geburah of Malkuth)

The mental urge towards organisation and strategy making. The energy of purposeful action targeting growth and advancement. The mind-set of "I will...".

The Seventh Gate (Chesed of Malkuth)

Emotional bonding. Sympathy for others in a state of suffering. The emotional seat of our humanity and the root of our capacity for Family and Self love.

The Eighth Gate (Binah of Malkuth)

The seat of Intelligence. The gate that is entered by our ability to learn from experience.

The Ninth Gate (Chokmah of Malkuth)

This gate may be accessed by our ability to make informed choices. Self-trust.

The Tenth Gate (Kether of Malkuth)

The capacity for self experience and self awareness. The source of the intensity of orgasm rising as a response to the 'lower' inspirations of that event.

The Nine Gates of Yesod:

The 'higher' gates may only be intimated through allegory and parable as they lie beyond the remit of physical-sensual associations.

The Eleventh Gate (Yesod of Yesod)

Mulla Kif came across four wise men seated cross legged before the rising Sun.

"We have been sitting here in stillness all night, awaiting the dawn," said one of the men. Another man farted.

Pointing to the sky, the Mulla said: "Look, it has come and gone. The dawn waits not for the prophet who seeks to enter the city on his ass but does not have the sense to move his bowels."

The Twelfth Gate (Hod of Yesod)

The Mulla came upon a wandering holy man, walking in the purple shades of the city walls. A retinue followed in the priest's wake and his disciples approached the Mulla with their bowls outstretched, seeking alms.

"Be gone," the good Mullah exhorted. "I am walking here to escape my worse nature. That does not mean that I am any better friend to my good nature. Tell me, if I give you what I have, what will you do with it?"

"We will feed the hungry. We will clothe the poor," they replied.

"But will I then not be hungry? Will I not be poor?" the Mulla asked.

And the followers saw the wisdom of his argument and turned upon their leader with angry words and abandoned him.

When they were gone, the Holy Man approached the Mullah and said: "Thank you, master. I've been trying to get rid of those bums for nigh on six months now."

The Thirteenth Gate (Netzach of Yesod)

A disciple came to Mulla Kif seeking guidance.

"Master," he implored, "I am always slipping into evil and doing things that I later regret. Help me."

The Mulla placed a hand on his shoulder, saying to the man: "If you are always running towards your shadow, my son, then you will find it is because you are running away from the light."

The Fourteenth Gate (Tiphareth of Yesod)

Two Angels were waiting on the corner of the street where the Mulla lived. One wore a black cloak, the other a white one.

When the Mulla came out of his house he saw the Angels waiting for him at the end of the road.

Turning his collar against the wind he set off in the opposite direction muttering to himself: "When Angels are to be found hustling on street corners, it is time to seek spirituality in the bordello.

The Fifteenth Gate (Geburah of Yesod)

A young man came upon a very old man sitting by the side of the path warming his hands on the flames of a small fire he had built. Sitting down by his side he offered him a drink from his flask and a few figs from his canteen.

After many pleasantries the old man said: "When I was young I was a disciple of the Mulla, but I ran away. It is something that I deeply regret."

The young man enquired: "Why did you turn aside from the Mullah's wisdom?"

The old man replied: "I had been a novice for one whole year, and I approached the Mulla asking him to tell me the name of my higher angel. He whispered the name in my ear, but I was too young to understand his answer and thought he was tricking me, so I left."

"What name did he tell you, old man?" The young man enquired.

"It was my own name," the old man sighed.

The Sixteenth Gate (Chesed of Yesod)

Kif appeared in the market square amongst the crowds who had gathered to listen to the Christian prophets of doom speak of the end of the world. Upon his back he carried a parachute.

His friend Ali saw him approaching and cried: "Kif, why do you wear a parachute?"

"I met a chicken and a turkey on the road here, and they told me that the sky was falling," Kif replied.

"The prophets here speak of the end of the world," Ali said sombrely. "They say that anyone who reads their Bible and believes will be saved."

"Well," said Kif, "you will be safe if you buy their book. I am safe, because I have my parachute. But I cannot believe that God will not spare the chicken and the turkey."

The Seventeenth Gate (Binah of Yesod)

Kif came across the desert and beheld the pyramids for the first time.

A veiled woman came out of the shadow of the sphinx to greet him. Beneath her coat she held a desert fox, veiling it from the morning winds.

"Girl," Kif called out, "I am following the stars looking for three Kings."

Pointing to a row of three small pyramids she said: "You have found them. But they have been long dead."

"Still, I will sleep here and pass the night with them," Kif said, dismounting from his camel.

"Sir," the veiled maiden addressed him. "You are the first who has passed this way who has not been overwrought with sorrow at finding the objects of his quest so long deceased."

"I came this way because I believed the stars were calling me to be here at this time. I will lie beneath the stars at this place and seek their wisdom in dreams. Would you care for some fresh water and figs?" Kif asked politely, offering the girl his canteen and flask.

"Sir, your chivalry does you proud," she replied. "But it is written that at a time such as this, one like yourself might give all for a kiss but "whosoever gives one particle of dust shall lose all at that hour."

Recognising her as a priestess of Nuit, goddess of the night sky, Kif bowed his head. "Madam," he said, "you are certainly welcome to all and everything I possess."

Dropping her veil, the priestess revealed herself to Kif and they kissed under the desert skies.

"You are indeed a fool, if you plan to continue through the desert," the priestess said gently. "Here, take this little desert fox. It will guide you through the wilderness and warn you of the scorpions in the dark of night. You have broken the letter and the spirit of the law of the holy book this night in kissing me. But your audacity weighs in balance with your kindness, and this puts you beyond our blessing or forgiveness. Journey on, noble traveller. But follow the dog," and she passed him the desert fox and departed.

The Eighteenth Gate (Chokmah of Yesod)

An acolyte came to the Mulla, saying: "Take me as your pupil, O master. I would do anything to prove myself worthy."

"Then take this box to the Mulla who lives over the river", Kif said, handing him an old shoe box tied firmly with string. "But do not look inside, or I will know you are unworthy."

All through the journey, a voice cried out from the box: "May Allah save us! May Allah save us!" As he was crossing the river, the acolyte's curiosity became too much for him and he loosened the string and peeked inside.

As soon as he opened the box a parrot flew out, fell into the river and was washed away.

Returning to the Mulla, he confessed himself, begging forgiveness and a second chance to make amends.

The Mulla pointed to the temple door.

"Be gone!" he said. "You show more respect for the voice of a parrot than for the commands of your teacher. If I taught you in the Law you would become more of a policeman than a judge!"

The Nineteenth Gate (Kether of Yesod)

"I am knowing, and yet rarely known." The Goddess said to Kif in his dream. "If you would know me, you must sit in the deepest well in the city for three nights at the dark of the Moon." So Kif purchased an oversize bucket and had himself lowered into the well the next day.

The people of the town were amazed and a large crowd gathered around to witness his vigil. For three days and nights Kif remained in the well. To his surprise he found that he could see the stars of the heavens in the day time as well as at night. And so he became dumb-struck with awe.

When he was hauled up, Kif was summoned to the tent of the Caliph, who wished to learn what Kif had experienced down the well, and offered a meal and wine.

Refusing these, Kif requested a simple bowl of dates and a glass of goats milk which he consumed with relish. He was then brought before the Caliph who asked him: "What did the Goddess reveal of Herself to you, my son?"

Kif stared at him for a moment before replying. "In seeking the light, we are all blinded by it," he said. "It is what is beyond the light that should concern us: for the light shines out of a darkness which cradles us continuously.

"The Light is the Way, but the darkness is the beginning and the end."

"And how may we know the Goddess? How is it that we may come to know the unknowable?" The Caliph further pursued.

"By living simple lives," Kif replied. "And by learning that one must descend into the darkness in order to see beyond the light."

The Eight Gates of Hod

The Twentieth Gate (Hod of Hod)

Coconut was selling figs in the market square one morning when a travelling master magician and hypnotist arrived and set up his stage next to his pitch.

Throughout the morning crowds gathered to see the hypnotist convince men that they were donkeys, and women that they were tigers. Stupid men came to be cured of their imbecility, those with stutters were made able to speak clearly, the lame walked and the nearly blind were restored to sight. As the crowds gathered, Coconut sold more figs in one morning than he might reasonably expect to do in a week or more. Counting his takings with deep satisfaction, Coconut decided that he would make a habit of following the magician from town to town.

Towards the end of the morning as noon came upon them, each of the stall holders closed for the mid day heat break.

The hypnotist counted his gold, paid to him by those seeking to be hypnotised. Having sold his entire stock of figs Coconut counted his money too, and made up his mind to consult the hypnotist himself when the afternoon session began.

Haven taken his place in the queue, Coconut's turn soon came about and the Master hypnotist asked him what he wished of him.

"I wish to marry an intelligent woman, who will give me strong and clever children," Coconut replied. "But I fear that I am too poor and simple to be of interest to such a bride."

"And what would you give for this?" the hypnotist enquired.

"Oh, I would give anything to lead a fulfilling life," Coconut replied. "I would follow you and pay you a share of my profits if you could make such a thing possible.

"Then promise me a share in your business equal to one third and I will grant your wishes," the hypnotist commanded, and so Coconut agreed to give over a third share of his business profits to the Master.

After placing the fig-seller in a deep hypnotic trance the Master commanded him to be wise in all dealings, discerning in all purchases, fair with all people and cheerful against all adversity. Then he put his mouth to Coconuts ear and, in a whisper, commanded him to take all of his powers from him.

When Coconut awoke from his trance he found that he knew many things that he previously did not and that everyone that he spoke to treated him with deference and respect; obeying his will even so far as paying immediate attention to his slightest wants, needs, or casual suggestions.

And as the afternoon passed, Coconut began to recollect more and more about his consultation with the Master Hypnotist, who had suddenly shut up his stall immediately after treating him.

Remembering that he had pledged one third of his business to the master hypnotist, Coconut turned to a near by merchant in fine cloths whom he had seen arrive with other traders in the retinue of the master hypnotists caravan.

"I have given a third share in my business to the Master," Coconut exclaimed. "And he has given me a share of his powers. I do not understand."

"There are many merchants in the Master's caravan," the silk merchant answered. "And in this town, at this time, we have need of figs. If you follow the master as one of our number, as now you must, you will always show a profit on your figs. And you will not even need to work your stall, for the Master will provide willing servants to do the work of the donkey."

"And what will I do?" Coconut hesitantly enquired.

"You will do the work of the Master entertaining the masses and curing the sick," the merchant replied. "You now have the power to do anything you so desire. But in this one thing you must now abide."

"But all I wanted was an intelligent and good looking wife," Coconut protested.

"You can have your pick of wives," the merchant answered, "they will come running at your bidding. You are now the Master and the power has been passed on to you."

"Truly has the weight of responsibility fallen on my shoulders," Coconut muttered. "But why do you say I will have to be crafty?"

"Well, you know the Master who hypnotised you?" the Merchant asked. Coconut nodded his head. "Well, when he had the power passed on to him do you know what he asked for?"

Coconut shook his head. The merchant continued: "Well, he wanted to go into the fig business."

The Twenty First Gate (Netzach of Hod)

Marah went wandering in the western lands, where the priests studied the stars at night.

Alone, save for the company of the camel upon whose back she rode, she travelled between the oases of the desert; seeking the stillness of the night time to heal her troubled soul.

In the evening she hunted with a bow and arrow for food. In the morning she lay down in the shade of the palms of the oasis and dreamed through the day.

One day whilst she slept, Marah dreamed a strange dream: Two headless men faced one another over a net stretched across a black and white chequered ball-court. They were throwing a dismembered head to one another. The head was screaming.

Troubled by this dream, Marah sought the company of the priests who wandered the desert at night, examining the skies through their tripod devices. Seeking the elder of the priests Marah told him of her dream.

"My Child," he replied, "you are troubled in your soul. "There are two rival forces at work within you - the affirming and the denying force. Your mind and your heart are at odds."

"That is why I wander the desert at night," she replied, "singing the song of the night wind, seeking a star to guide me."

The old priest smiled. "We are all creatures of the day time," he said. "Why do you not seek the light of the star that gives us nourishment by day?"

The lady paused before replying: "A Sufi once told me that more people are blinded by the light than are enlightened by it. In any case, I am a child of the desert. The day star would burn me to a crisp if I were to wander about in the noon heat."

"Then you should take yourself unto prayer at dawn and at the time when the Sun is setting," the old priest replied. "The darkest night and the brightest day are not for you."

And so the lady of the desert took his words to heart and followed his advice for the remainder of her days.

At night, before dawn, the scorpions of the desert ran about her feet and she took care to do them no harm; languishing in the beauty of life emergent.

In the dawning hours of the desert day time, she took comfort in the little flowers that sprang up beneath the rocks of long forgotten cities; languishing in the beauty of life emergent.

And as the years passed, after she had breathed her last breath, the star goddess noticed the shadow of the desert daughter's memory passing across the oceans of sand. And the Lady of Night took her into the heavens to shine as a star upon the world in the evenings and the mornings to wander the tapestry of the firmament for an eternity.

And, for a brief while, the mystery of this lady's passing may be seen before the sunrise and after the sunset. And in her rising and setting lies the mystery of our evolution.

So thus it is that the wise Men of Earth take themselves unto meditation at the times of dawn and dusk; avoiding the darkest night and the brightest day.

The Twenty Second Gate (Tiphareth of Hod)

One day, an infinite number of horse drawn coaches began arriving at Hilbert's Hotel carrying an infinite number of passengers seeking a bed for the night.

Luckily the Hotel was empty and had an infinite number of rooms, and so the travellers were accommodated easily. A few hours later another infinite number of horse drawn coaches could be seen on the horizon carrying a further infinite number of passengers seeking shelter.

The hotel manager scratched his head in bewilderment and sought advice from Kif, the local holy man whom he knew to be never far away from the Hotel kitchens after the evening call to prayer had been answered.

The wily old priest pondered the problem for a few moments and then began beating the hotel manager about the head with his prayer shawl.

"You are a Fool to bother me with such a problem," he said. "Simply move all the guests you have staying with you to even numbered rooms, and put the new arrivals in the odd numbered ones."

The Twenty Third Gate (Geburah of Hod)

Kif was visiting a village at the foot of the mountains near the desert where a famous worker of wonders taught his disciples the secrets of magick and walking through fire.

When the fakir heard that the great Sufi Kif was praying at the temple in his village he sent his chief disciples to invite the learned sage to a feast that would be held in his honour that same evening.

Kif arrived at the celebrations and took his place at he head of the table beside his host. Fatted calves and lambs had been slaughtered and laid before the company. Dancing girls entertained the assembly between courses, and the fakir's disciples waited upon the two learned ones throughout the banquet.

As the light grew dim, the chatter of conversation filled the temple. Kif and the worker of wonders had exchanged no more words than a simple greeting at the commencement of the proceedings and sat next to one another in silence. When the bowls were being cleared from the floor the fakir clapped his hands together and his pupils prepared the fire pit for a demonstration of their skill.

After an hour, the flaming embers were judged to be ready for the demonstration and, one by one, the wonder worker's disciples walked the length of the pit of flames apparently untouched by the heat.

The crowd applauded each of them as they completed their walk. As the last disciple completed his demonstration, Kif asked the fakir how he trained his followers to perform such wonders.

"By meditation upon the chapters of the Holy Book." The fakir replied.

Upon hearing these words Kif took a particularly valuable copy of the Holy Book from his robes and cast them into the flames, burning the tome to cinders.

"This is sacrilege," the followers of the wonder worker cried. "Kif must die for his crime." And they swept him aloft in their arms and cast him into the fire.

After lying there for a few minutes, Kif rose to his feet unscathed and looked upon the angry crowd whereupon a deep silence fell over them. His gaze was as cold as ice, and the assembly began to know fear.

"He is a demon," some of them cried.

"Look, the fire has not touched him," others shouted.

"You are wrong," Kif said, remonstrating with them. "The fire of the spirit is more fierce than the fire that springs from wood or earth. Behold....." he reached down into the flames and pulled out the Holy Book which, moments before had been destroyed in the flames. And with this he strode out of the burning pit.

"It is a trick," the fakir exclaimed. "You must be a demon. You were not prepared for the fire, and yet you are untouched by the flames."

Kif seized the wonder worker by the throat. "You are a deceiver." he said. "It is you who are the spawn of darkness, for you have taught your disciples to work parlour tricks from meditations upon the sacred verses in the name of the Most High." And with that, he cast the deceiver into the fire whereupon he was consumed.

At once, the disciples of the former fakir surrounded Kif and begged him to tell them how he had managed to destroy the deceiver with the same fire the fakir had taught them could not hurt the righteous and which he had faced many times before in demonstration of his power.

"And tell us Master, how you managed to reclaim the Holy book from the flames," one disciple beseeched him.

"The letters of the Law are written in celestial flame and cannot be destroyed by earthly fire," Kif replied. "For the law is written in flame upon the heart of those who love it and can never truly be lost.

"Your master was consumed by the flame of the spirit which resides within the law. It was the flame of righteousness that destroyed him. Before the Holy book burned before you, the fire of the pit was merely the fire of earthly destruction which the law was given to save you from."

"Then should we burn our Books of the Law?" the disciples enquired. "To liberate ourselves from the ashes of the world?"

"Yes." Kif replied. "But you should burn the Book of the Law in the furnace of experience. Do not take a match to it. Until its words are scorched into your hearts and minds, you will continue to live in the realm of shadow.

"In order to see the world clearly you must become the light. Then, even the letters of the Law will seem as shadows to you for you will have become the Law."

"And how will we know when we are truly at one with the Law?" The disciples asked him.

"When someone takes offence at your actions and tries to burn you at the stake as a heretic," Kif replied. "If the flames do not touch you, then you are indeed enlightened."

And from that day Kif became known as Lord Flame.

Note: Samuel Johnson was known as the Gawsworth Jester, and commonly as Maggoty Johnson.. In addition to being the last professional jester in England his success lay as an actor and playwright. His pseudonym was 'Lord Flame', the central character in his own play *Hurlothrumbo* which ran for 50 nights at the Haymarket in London.

He lies buried in a spinney called 'Maggoty Johnson's Wood' - approximately 5 kilometres south west of Macclesfield, England alongside the A536.

The Twenty Fourth Gate (Chesed of Hod)

Kif departed from the feast with his servant Kilo, who awaited him within the shadows of the Temple gate and left the village for the city. The night was dark and only the brightest stars could be seen twinkling in the firmament above the mountain peaks.

On the way home Kilo, who had been a long time pupil and valued confidant of the Sufi joked with him as was his privilege: "You know, I think that it might just be possible to talk one's way out of any situation, so long as one has studied the right books."

Kif remained silent but stopped, leaning on his staff, and regarded his companion with some amusement.

"I meant no offence, Master," Kilo replied, half smiling.

Kif reached into his robes and withdrew two lengths of thread. "One of these is white and one is black," he said, holding each length by one end from each hand. "Is the black thread on the left side or the right side?"

Kilo's smile spread a little wider. Holding up the index finger of his left hand and wagging it from side to side, he said: "You know that I have studied the Koran, Master. And it is written that such a judgment may not be made until the instant of Dawn.

"Choose anyway," the Mulla commanded.

"The black thread is on the left side," Kilo said confidently.

"And if I told you that it was on the right?" Kif enquired.

"Then I would tell you that you are looking at it from the wrong side," Kilo said, laughing.

"Why do you choose black on the left?" Kif asked.

"Black is wise," Kilo stated, now deadly serious.

"And if I told you that both threads were white?"

Kilo said: "Then I would pray that the merciful Allah should not turn aside from the blind."

Kif smiled and passed Kilo his staff. "Indeed you have learned well. I pass my authority on to you, my pupil," he stated solemnly. "I go now into the desert to seek the city of pyramids. If we meet again it will be in the lands beyond. You will have no need of the staff there."

"I understand," Kilo whispered, embracing his former master in farewell. "Do you have any final words of advice for me?"

Kif broke free and walked a few paces towards the desert. Stopping and turning to face the new master, Kif regarded him for a few moments before speaking:

"Always carry two Books of the Law." he said. "If you never have need of them to get you out of a fix, you can always use them for crushing Beetles." And then he disappeared towards the beckoning shadows of the desert.

The Twenty Fifth Gate (Binah of Hod)

After forty days and nights Kif came to the Sphinx. A dark man sat beneath the great beast's gaze, smoking a hookah pipe. "You may go no further until you smoke with me and answer my riddle," he said.

Kif sat down beside him and started toking on the pipe. "Begin," he said.

"I am within the circle and without," the dark man began. "I have six sides, twelve edges and seek to impose my order on all things. What am I?"

Holding down a particularly satisfying draught of smoke for a moment, Kif thought deeply. As he exhaled a smile came over his face. "You are only half the story," he said wisely.

And with that both men burst into laughter.

"Pass on my friend." the dark man said offering Kif a small packet. "And here is your green passport to share with the Wise."

The Twenty Sixth Gate (Chokmah of Hod)

A beggar was the first to see Kilo enter the city dressed in the robes of his former master. Every so often the new Sufi would stop and look behind him before continuing.

The beggar approached him and, receiving alms, enquired what it might be that the Master was looking behind him for.

"I am looking for my followers," the Mulla explained before continuing on his way.

The beggar thought this to be most amusing and followed the Sufi at a discreet distance, telling friends who he met on the way about the predicament of the Master.

Every so often someone would similarly enquire of the Mullah why it was that he kept looking behind him, and receive the same answer as the beggar. They too would follow the Sufi telling their friends along the way, and very soon hundreds of others had joined the growing throng.

Before long Kilo reached the temple and the head priest beheld the approaching mass with the Sufi at its head, turning every few steps to regard the crowd before continuing.

The high priest met him at the gateway and enquired: "Master you are welcome. But why do you turn to look behind you so often?"

"I am looking for my followers," Kilo replied softly.

"But they seem to be many," the High Priest said. "Why do you so concern yourself?"

"The problem lies in distinguishing the Followers from the hangers-on," Kilo said with a thin smile. And with that he led the assembly into the outer court of the Temple and began to preach.

The Twenty Seventh Gate (Kether of Hod)

Kilo began to tell a fable to those who had come to hear him speak: "There was once a King who decided to share his power with nine worthy subjects who became his most trusted ministers.

"As the years went by the King grew further and further distant from the lives of his subjects. Affairs of State were looked after by the ministers and he found himself in need of stimulation.

"He took to dressing in old clothes and slipping out of the palace at night to mingle with his subjects in the taverns in his disguise. Returning to his chambers in the palace before dawn by a secret entrance he was not missed, but one day the King's first minister oversaw his comings and going and guessed the truth of the situation.

"This minister was a Republican and saw an opportunity to rid the country of the King and seize power himself. So he waited until the King took himself out into the taverns the next night and secured the secret entrance with locks and bolts so that the King might not return.

"The next morning, upon his return to the palace, the King found that he could not gain admittance and so presented himself to the palace guard at the main gate who turned him away with expressions of disbelief and derisory threats.

"Whilst the King sat in taverns and coffee houses planning his next course of action the Ministers declared him to be dead and the people wept.

"Months passed and the country began to fall into disarray under the evil dictatorship of the ministers. As taxes rose the people became discontented and suffered hardship. As the King continued in his disguise he came upon more and more people who recognised his wisdom and sought his counsel.

Those who shared their problems with him and did as he suggested soon recovered their prosperity and as the months passed into years the King found his counsel sought out by people of increasing affluence and power; each of whom came to respect his opinions and prospered through heeding it.

Soon the state of the country's economy grew so impoverished that the people rose up and overthrew the evil ministers. The priests and merchants and men of influence all sought the counsel of the King, whose reputation was now widespread.

Whilst he entertained the assembly of the learned and the powerful, the King cast off his disguise and told his story whereupon they swept him aloft and bore him to the palace."

Kilo finished his story and a silence settled upon the people who had heard him speak.

The Seven Gates of Netzach

The Twenty Eighth Gate (Netzach of Netzach)

The widow of the lost Prophet wandered in a garden she had once chanced upon, whilst walking in the Citadel. The garden was luscious with fauna and the flowers that grew there were wild and brightly coloured.

Forty different species of bird flourished in the garden, Leah had counted them, noting each by its song. She came here to meditate at morning and twilight every day, seeking consolation in the tranquillity of the garden's beauty.

Every day a different representative of each of the species of birds thatdwelt in the garden's trees and bushes flew down to sing to her. And as the days passed she grew to understand when the birds were singing to raise her spirits and when they were singing in conversation between themselves.

One day, lulled into a dreamy silence by the heady smell of white poppy leaves, Leah fell asleep for a while in the garden. When she awoke she found that she could understand the Language of the Birds, and everything that they were saying to one another.

After listening for a while, Leah sat up. From the important things that the birds had been discussing Leah realised that the garden she was sitting in was a meeting place of high council for the birds. The topics which the birds were discussing were wide and varied: How the winds were blowing, how much rain had fallen in the valleys and upon the mountains, how the crops were growing in the fields and how the seasons were subtly shifting in their pattern and duration.

A large peacock wandered over to sit before Leah, politely lowering it's brightly coloured tail. "How are you this morning, my lady?" the bird enquired. "Are you ready to converse with us, yet?"

"I would be delighted." Leah replied, having had time to compensate for the absurdity of the situation. "I have only this morning begun to understand your language. Please forgive my previous ignorance, if you have been trying to engage me in conversation before now."

"You are welcome here, Madam," the peacock continued. "This is our Parliament. Each of us have a different tale to tell, and we meet here to share stories and concerns. We have noticed your twice daily meditations in our garden and recognise the loss that lies within you. Tell me fair lady, what is the shadow that veils your heart?"

"My husband is lost to me, O mighty lord of the birds," Leah replied. "He has taken himself in search of the celestial City of Pyramids, where the Stars make their home upon the Earth far beyond the mountains and the desert sands. The people say he has disappeared forever and treat me as a widow. Even now, a new prophet sits in his place at the Temple."

"Fear not," the peacock replied, "news of your husband has reached our ears. He is descending from the mountains even now and approaches his intended destination. However, many surprises still lie ahead of him."

"Then he is truly lost to me for ever," Leah wailed.

"Be not overcome with grief," the peacock commanded, "your husband will indeed return to you, if only to take you beyond the desert to return with him to the City of Pyramids."

"How do you know this?" Leah enquired.

"It is evident to us that he must return," the peacock explained. "It is something of a riddle, well known to the wise, that no man may enter the City without his wife just as no woman may enter without her husband. And then only the child may enter."

"I do not understand," Leah stated.

"It is a riddle of the heart," said the peacock, "not of the head."

"Then how long must I await his return?" Leah asked.

"You must dwell within our garden for forty days and forty nights in order to prepare yourself for the journey," the peacock said. "We will guard the entrance from all intruders, so that you will be free of all distraction. You must sleep here naked, eating only from the fruit trees which grow here, and every night one of us will tell you a tale until you have heard each of the forty tales we have to tell."

"And what will I do when the forty days and nights have passed?" she enquired.

"It is not what you must do," the bird said solemnly. "It is what you will have become: a source of inspiration and secret lore which you may pool with your returning husband so that you may complete the journey beyond infinity successfully together. He will not be too long in returning, for we believe him to be truly wise. The path that he is treading leads ultimately to the valley of small circles, and there he will realise that he can proceed no further alone. He will return, do not fear."

And so Leah stripped herself of all her clothes and settled herself down in the luscious grasses of the garden to pass the forty days and nights in conversation with the birds and await her husband's return.

The Twenty Ninth Gate (Tiphareth of Netzach)

It was a tradition within the citadel that the ascending High Priest should either marry the wife of the vacating High Priest or else take himself a wife from the sacred prostitutes in the temple brothel if she should prove unwilling or had died.

Leah, the wife of Kif the lost prophet, had mysteriously disappeared from the streets of the citadel and could not be found for the ceremony and so Kilo took himself to the vestal virgins of the temple to seek a mate.

The chamber of harlots lay behind a veiled screen in the Holy of Holies within the heart of the temple. This portal was guarded by two vestal virgins, one of whom would enter the chamber to become a temple prostitute herself whenever a bride was purchased for a night of pleasure and released to be given the freedom of the city the following morning.

Not every maiden within the citadel became a temple prostitute, but those that did serve the temple in this way were free to choose any husband for themselves from the men of the citadel. The choice of a time-served Harlot was binding and no man could refuse to take her as one of his wives once he had been chosen. This meant that each of the priestesses of pleasure were able to choose husbands wisely once they had fulfilled their obligations to their divine office. Many of the girls married princes or merchants once they had spent the night with a worshipper. Sometimes, married women chose to return to service within the chamber in order to gain the right to choose a second or third husband. The vestal virgins of the temple were often only symbolically virginal. Both worship and service within the chamber of harlots were regarded by the people of the Citadel as rites of rebirth and spiritual renewal.

When Kilo slipped quietly into the temple of pleasure, the entire population held it's breath for this was an occasion of great expectation. The bride which Kilo would choose to 'marry' for the night would gain great respect and influence, and she would be greatly prized as a wife by any man whom she chose to take as a husband after laying down with the High Priest.

In the morning, when the wedding night was over and the warm aura of conjugal bliss settled over the waking High Priest and his chosen bride, they fell into conversation together. Marah, whom Kilo had chosen to take unto himself, was named after the mighty ocean upon whose shores she had grown up as a girl. She began to tell him of her life as a fishing girl, of her hopes and aspirations and of her thirst for knowledge and stimulating companionship.

"And whom will you choose for a husband?" Kilo enquired of her.

"There is a boy in my home village outside of the Citadel, whom I always thought I would like to marry," she replied. "He is clever and quick witted, and also the son of the tribal chief."

"And will you bless him with a proposal of marriage?" Kilo asked.

"No," Marah answered. "There comes a point when we have to leave something of our lives behind, if we are to move on to fresh challenges. If I had slept for one night with anyone other than you the High Priest, then I think that I would indeed have returned to marry him."

"Then what will you do?" Kilo said.

"I will remain as I am." Marah replied. "I married you last night, and so do not technically need to seek a husband in the world. Having married, I am already a free woman and the fee I have earned from my service to you last night will enable me to enjoy my life in the world. I think that I will remain here in the temple by night and move freely about the world by day.

You may visit me whenever you will, for you must now regard me as your wife having taken me as such during your dutiful obligations to your high office.

"A wife of the High Priest remaining in the Chamber of Harlots?" Kilo cried. "This is most unusual."

"It is the way it must be." Marah replied. "You have made me a free woman, and yet I would continue to be your wife in spirit. We have known the best of both worlds, and it is my right to choose you as a husband and a lover if I so wish."

And so Marah became the wife of Kilo the High Priest from that moment on and was allowed to continue to return to her chamber within the Temple at her leisure.

And Marah was known and respected throughout the land from that day hence as having made the wisest of choices.

The Thirtieth Gate (Geburah of Netzach)

Cast out from the citadel the Purple Sage took himself unto the hills, following the footprints in the sand. A smile played upon his lips as he looked down upon the lands to which he would never return.

By chance he had stumbled across the long lost secret formula of power which his order had sought for nigh on twelve centuries now.

He had been making love to a temple prostitute of the Order of Nuit when the value and significance of all human life became apparent to him and transformed his understanding of the world.

Everyone who knew him sensed the change within him and it became whispered that he had stumbled across the secret of all existence.

The august brotherhood, of which the Purple Sage had once been a trusted member, had employed Astrologers to seek the lost wisdom in the stars; Alchemists to reveal its hiding place within the secret metals of the Earth; Qabalists to search for it within the leaves of dusty tomes and numerous other learned sages from both East and West.

Twice yearly the Wise Ones took counsel together and debated the significance of their discoveries. The citadel was always busy around these times and travellers arrived from distant lands to hear the wise men speak. It was the duty of each citizen of the citadel to speak at this Council and everyone awaited the turn of the Purple Sage.

It was at one of these conventions that the Purple Sage arose from his seat to address the gathering.

"I have found the secret lore," he declared, "and I wish to reveal my findings to the learned." A great commotion arose amongst the crowd and heads turned to behold him. The chairman of the meeting beckoned the Purple Sage towards the speaker's podium, and as he ascended the steps of the lectern an expectant hush fell over the assembly.

The Purple Sage was about to speak of his understanding of the great mystery when Coco the Learned, Master of the Qabalah, spoke out in a loud voice: "Tell us, before you speak of the Mysteries O Purple Sage, how long you worked in pursuit of the ultimate conundrum before you resolved the mystery?"

In a faltering voice, the Purple Sage declared that his revelation had come to him in an instant and that it had been so crystal clear that he had immediately seized upon its meaning."

"The work of an instant!" The Qabalistic master declared facetiously. "And our fore fathers have struggled in pursuit of the secret for untold centuries." And with these words, he departed the chamber shaking his head from side to side.

Before the Purple Sage could formulate a reply, another Master spoke out. This time it was Lassid, the Mystic: "And what spiritual exercises were you pursuing to lead you to this enlightenment?" he enquired.

"I was working on a new approach," the Purple Sage declared. "You see, the traditional systems have failed us thus far; for they have not allowed us to even begin to ask the right questions."

At these words Lassid let out a roar and departed from the chamber taking his followers with him.

The questions continued, thick and fast: "Where were you when the answer came to you?"

"In the arms of a beautiful priestess of the Temple of Nuit!"

"How can you verify your vision according to the lore of the Temple philosophers?"

"The secret does not reside within the Temple, but may be found in the Outer Court by any passing stranger!"

"Tell us of the riddle of the Egg in the desert?"

"I do not think that you are capable of understanding the secret lore if you continue to phrase the Mysteries in terms of clichés," he replied.

"You do not speak to us in plain words," one Master objected.

"You ask riddles of me but will not let me speak freely!" the Purple Sage replied. But the crowd continued to question, heckle and desert him as they grew angry at his answers and as time passed the Purple Sage grew tired of the criticism from the floor and retired to his seat, signalling to all that he would say no more.

Those that had remained to hear his revelation then grew angry with him in frustration and the crowd rose up as one and threw him out of the meeting hall; mocking him and heaping upon his shoulders the indignity of rejection.

Now at that time there was a gateway in the city walls that had never been used in the entire history of the citadel. Legend and folk lore had grown up around this gateway. Some said that the Chosen One would pass through it. Some claimed that it could only be opened by the angels. Some stories claimed that the gate led to higher realms, and that those who passed through it would never be seen again.

It had remained closed since the days of the mighty engineers, students of the Old Magicians who had planned the architecture of the Citadel according to the principles of the celestial harmonies of the Universe. It was to this gate that the mocking assembly led the Purple Sage.

Laughing and cajoling him with sarcasm and unkind remarks they challenged him to open the gate. "If you have truly achieved enlightenment, then you must prove it." One of them said with a bitter laugh.

"You are fools." the Purple Sage said. Stepping forward, he laid his palm flat against the stone face of the gateway and simply pushed and stepped through the portal into the light. He was never seen in the Citadel again. For many centuries after this, every word of the Purple Sage's replies to the Wise Men's questions were analysed, argued over and discussed. New Qabalistic theosophies were interpreted in his words and novel systems of lateral thinking grew up based around the implications of his passing through the gate of no return.

But every so often, a young novitiate would pass unseen into the temple of Nuit by a secret door and would return to slip surreptitiously out of the citadel by means of the gate through which the Purple Sage had passed.

And these exits went unnoticed by the many for the servants of the star goddess are few and secrete their wisdom gently from this world in a manner beyond whispers and allusion.

The Thirty First Gate (Chesed of Netzach)

The Bell

Far across the desert and through the night they had ridden, these dusty pilgrims, driving their camels hard in pursuit of the new star.

Caked in the white sands of the desert basins they paused to honour the rising sun whilst their retinue struggled to keep pace.

Two days ride ahead lay the Mountains of Madness, beyond which the fabled City of Pyramids dominated the western lands. One of the camel masters pointed and shouted to the mounted pilgrims: "One hour's journeying hence, and we shall find the oasis which we seek."

The leader of the white riders grunted, then signalled for the preparations for the adoration of the rising Sun to begin.

The travellers dismounted and raised their arms towards the sun. Leaning their heads slightly to the left they intoned:

"Hail unto thee who art Ra in thy rising.

Even unto thee who art Ra in thy strength.

Who travels over the heavens in thy bark,

at this the uprising of the Sun.

Tahuti standeth at the helm

and Ra Hoor abideth at the prow.

Hail unto thee from the abodes of Night!"

By the time they arrived at the oasis the sun was still low in the sky. A team of camels laden with silks for the eastern markets plodded towards them, led by a small group of merchants riding in a sheltered wagon. As the caravan of the star seekers passed by them in single file the camel master raised his closed fist in traditional greeting and, as the last of the merchant's camels departed from the palm rich oasis, the first of the pilgrims arrived there.

A solitary figure, clad in the dark black and purple of the holy man sat watching the approaching caravan from beneath one of the leafy palms. When the pilgrims had quenched their thirst from the spring waters of the oasis and their servants had erected the tents to protect their number from the rage of the desert sunlight, the leader of the star seekers sent his manservant to the holy man, inviting him to the hospitality of his tent for refreshment and counsel.

Kif accepted, and broke his fast in the tent of the eastern bound caravan with a meal of fruit and dates. "Where are you bound, holy man?" the leader enquired, once they had finished their simple meal.

"I am bound for the City of Pyramids," Kif replied.

"Then you are indeed walking a winding path," the leader commented. "We have roamed this desert for generations, and sometimes visit there. Some tales say that every man and woman, in some lifetime or another must pass through its gate."

"It is given to me to have that privilege," Kif stated. "I would be grateful to you if you would share your knowledge of the pathway which leads there and also tell me of your own quest."

It was the son of the pilgrim star seeker who replied to Kif, whilst refilling his guest's goblet with wine: "Who treads the path of the desert fox is a brother to us. Our camel master will set you upon the best path when you depart. But let me speak to you of our mission in the desert.

"We are musicians. That is our tradition. Our fathers and mothers sang with the desert winds at the raising of the pyramid city. We visit and sing with the running waters of the mighty rivers beyond the white sands: old songs, older than the songs we sing of the valleys and the plains. Our sagas tell the stories of the raising of the mountains; of the retreat of the great sea; of the coming of the sunlight and of the birth of the day.

"Once, every few generations, the heavens move and we sing with the stars and the Moon. We sing with the old stars, but sometimes there are new songs to learn and new stars to follow that we may catch their melody."

"You speak of the new star that rushes towards Jupiter?" Kif enquired.

"We do." The pilgrim leader answered, signalling for his son to refill his goblet. "It will collide with that mighty orb and be no more this very night."

"But it will sing a song in it's passing that will be remembered as the overture of a new Aeon," the leader's son continued. "We seek the place where our ancestors sang the song of the first star of the morning: the star of the goddess. She will hear the mighty song and whisper it in our ears whilst we lie in her secret place."

"The song of the shooting star will ring like a bell throughout the heavens," his father mused.

"May your songs continue to bring life to the world," Kif said with ritual solemnity. "I will hear your song in my dreams and pray to the gods of the heavens for the new awakening of the world."

"Now tell us if you have any need of anything that we may have to make your journey an easy one," the pilgrim leader said expansively. "You

will find that your arrival within the City of Pyramids may not be the end
of your journey. For there are many cities within the great city. Each
is a perfect representation of itself and only after many adventures there
can a man truly tell one from another and come at last to the true City
of Pyramids on the shore of the Great Sea."

Kif tried to refuse the hospitality of the camp, but fresh stores of fruit,
wine and bread were presented to him in a pack to ease his journey
beyond the mountains. The camel master gave him directions and Kif
bade farewell to the caravan with blessings and prayers of good fortune.

"Before you go, let me give you these tokens and words of advice." The
pilgrim leader said in parting. "Here is a hawk feather, and also the
feather of the peacock. They will serve as amulets of protection upon
the path which you must tread, and also as keys to present to guardians
who may question your right tread the path which we have set you
upon. Present them to any soul who questions you and you will pass
safely for they will know that the Watchers have sent you. But you may
have to give one up to a guardian, somewhere along the way.

"Remember there may be guides like ourselves, and guardians too upon
the path ahead: but no denizen of the desert is truly as he or she appears.
Follow your shadow from here on and you will come to the winding
pathway that must be climbed over the mountain range. Your shadow
will then be behind you, until you come to the city where no shadows
are cast."

"Farewell," Kif replied. "I will listen for your songs upon the desert
wind from those very mountains."

"And take this song in your heart, as you pass from us," the pilgrim
father said. He then began to hum a melody which his fellows took up
in chorus as the holy man began his trek into the desert, And that same
melody was upon his lips at one time or another during every day that
followed.

The Thirty Second Gate (Binah of Netzach)

Having climbed the winding path up the mountain range, Kif reached the summit and paused to regain his breath and refresh himself with a drink from his flask of wine. An old tree stood a little way down the descending slope ahead and Kif sat beneath it, his back to the wood.

His journey from the oasis had passed without incident. Once he thought that he was being watched by unseen eyes, but he had passed onwards through the mighty sand dunes looking neither to the right nor the left; fixing his gaze upon the Hawk and Peacock feathers which he held before him.

As he had approached the rising mountain range, leaving the desert sands behind him Kif thought that he heard voices calling his name. But he did not look back. Instead he fixed his attention firmly upon the song of the desert dwellers who sought after the song of the stars. Their parting melody was burned into his mind, having remained with him in a memory of hypnotic intensity since his journey from the oasis.

As he had climbed the winding pathway, the holy man caught the dull glimmer of ores of precious metals and the glint of gemstones only an arms reach from the rising natural stairwell. A treasure fit for a King might be bought for only a handful of these raw jewels, but Kif maintained his steady progress upwards.

Whilst he rested the light began to fade in the West, and the stars blinked and twinkled in the skies above. A carpet of light cloud lay a hundred feet beneath the Holy Man's feet, illuminated by the faint light of a rising crescent moon to the south. Kif sighed at the beauty of the still night and gently fell into a sleep.

When he awoke the heavens were bright with starlight. The Moon had arisen and was majestically creeping westward, but the lights surrounding the planet Jupiter directly above were spectacular. A rainbow haze lay around the planet and Kif thoughts were of the song which was now being sung by the star seekers.

As his eyes adjusted to their surroundings Kif became aware of a soft voice in his ear. It seemed to him that it was a deep female voice coming to him from far away and yet it spoke in a whisper.

Although he was not afraid, the Sufi clutched the Hawk and Peacock feathers tightly before him. "Do not be stirred to fear, gentle wanderer," the voice said softly. "I have sheltered you beneath my boughs in the hours of your slumber and kept you from all harm. You may trust me for I recognise the symbols which you bear, and honour their significance."

"O honourable Talking Tree," Kif addressed the nature spirit. "I recognise you as a guardian and greet you, with respect, as an equal."

"I am impressed by your keen insight," the Talking Tree replied, waving it's barren branches in the night breeze. "Now answer me two riddles if indeed you are an equal. If so you prove to be, you may pass unharmed but not unchanged."

"What is the test?" Kif demanded, recognising the ritual procedure from folk tales of old and adopting the formal etiquette of the occasion. "I will answer your riddles and meet wit with wit."

The tree was silent for a moment before answering. A hushed air of expectancy and drama had crept into the night time stillness. Then the nature spirit spoke:

"To gain what you seek, you must lose what you need. To pass by, you must remain where you stand. You must give up all to tread this pathway further. To make space for what you must find, you must be filled up with what I demand."

Kif stood in silent contemplation for a moment before replying: "To lose what I need and remain where I stand will involve me standing naked before you." He shed his outer robes until he was garbed in only a single light robe and sandals, stepping out from the crumpled silks to leave them where he had stood.

"It says in the Book of the Law that whosoever gives one particle of dust in such an hour shall lose all," the Sufi continued. "I will keep my sandals and under garment as is customary in such riddling matters, as I shall keep my pack.

"But, here," he said, offering something very small to the talking tree on the tip of his finger, "you may have this speck of dust. It is a crumb of the finest incense which I intended to burn to the Goddess. I now burn it to her in your name."

Reaching down, Kif took a charcoal block from his kit bag, lit a match and set it alight throwing the speck of incense upon it to smoulder and release it's perfume.

"And to be filled with what you demand," the Sufi continued, "would be to yield completely to the trust which you originally asked of me. So I will offer you one of these feathers as a token of exchange for my freedom to continue upon the path."

"You have spoken wisely and with great insight," the talking tree complimented him. "You have arrived at my second riddle. For I will ask you to choose which feather you shall present me with. Choose ye well, for it shall be the final challenge."

"O noble Lady!" Kif said worshipfully. "I recognise you now as the lady Nuit herself. For is it not written in your name ... because of my hair, the Trees of Eternity.... in the Book of the Law.

"I now recognise the feathers which I bear. The feather of the Kestrel Hawk, sacred to Horus your son, which would bring you comfort; and the feather of the Peacock Hen, sacred in the lands of the East to yourself and the Priestesses of your Temple, which would bring you honour."

And so Kif held out one of the feathers and placed it upon one of the talking tree's branches, whereupon leaves miraculously began to appear.

"You have done well to so choose." the talking tree said joyfully. In a matter of minutes the branches and boughs were fully obscured by the wealth of leaf growth and, as these rustled in the night wind it seemed to Kif as if he could see the face of a beautiful woman speaking to him in the shadows and shapes of the leaves as they moved too and fro in the moonlight. "Depart from here as you are. You shall only face one more challenge before you reach the end of your journey. You have shown both discrimination and sensitivity in your approach to the Mysteries, go now with my blessings."

And so Kif journeyed onwards.

The Thirty Third Gate (Chokmah of Netzach)

As Kif made his way down through the mountain woodland slopes towards the Eternal City he came upon the ruins of an ancient Temple. The dim yellow light of oil lamps could be seen burning from within the shell of the building, and the Sufi sensed shadows moving to and fro amidst the fallen masonry and decay.

Deciding to give the building a wide berth, Kif searched the perimeter of the clearing for a route whereby he might pass unnoticed. The pathways to both right and left were overgrown with bracken and the tangle of untamed branches, affording no easy passage. And so the Sufi gathered his wits about him and proceeded cautiously towards the building.

As Kif approached the main gateway of the ruin, a small man in Eastern style robes of peacock blue silk stepped into his path, his palm open and outstretched.

"You may pass no further, O Seeker." the man said gently. "Few pass this way, but those who do must take hospitality at this shrine and partake in the Ritual of the Serpent before they may continue."

"It seems that I have little choice but to obey." Kif replied, and the Mage led him within.

Seated upon the floor within the inner sanctum of the temple, Kif and the eastern sage faced each other over a low table. Coffee and dates were served by naked servants, male and female, with flaming red hair and wild green eyes. A Hookah pipe was brought to them whilst they drank, eying one another cautiously.

Kif guessed that the Temple guardian must be at least a hundred years old. His robes, though clean, looked the worse for wear and the Sufi had to examine them with a keen eye in order to behold the detail of the embroidered crescent moons and stars within their folds.

"The ritual of the serpent must now begin," the Mage announced, and two musicians stepped out from a curtain behind him; one holding a flute and one a lyre. A third man then stepped out, holding a basket which he carried to the table and there set it down.

The musicians took up a baleful drone of a melody, and the flame-haired servants lit a charcoal block and set it glowing within a copper bowl upon the table top. The third man who had entered then reached into the basket and pulled out a snake which Kif recognised to be highly venomous.

The man then began singing to the snake and stroking it until it became stiff and tranquil. Placing it upon the table top before the eastern Mage, the man drew a dagger from his own robes and swiftly chopped off the head of the snake. Kif continued to sit silently, sipping his coffee and carefully watching the proceedings.

The servants were busily filling the bowl of the pipe with hashish resin and opium poppies, and when they had finished the snake charmer placed the severed head of the serpent on the top of the pipe's bowl.

When these preparations were completed, the old temple guardian placed the burning charcoal block on top of the snake's head and replaced the cap of the bowl. Handing Kif one of the two mouthpieces attached to the pipe by red tubing the old man began to toke deeply from his own; inhaling the smoke deep into his lungs and then breathing out a voluminous cloud of smoke through his nostrils.

"You must take the breath of the serpent seven times before you may pass through this Temple," he said ceremoniously. "You must pause in meditation after drawing each draught."

And so Kif took his turn at the pipe, and as he did so the quality of the lighting within the chamber began to diminish in strength and the heady tones of the music swelled in his ears. After he had taken the first breath from the pipe a vision of his youth presented itself to Kif. He saw himself lying in the arms of a beautiful maiden whom he had loved as a young man. The bed they lay upon was adorned with leopard skins, and fabulous silks hung from the roof of the room in which they lay tangled in each others limbs.

The picture in Kif's mind then raced on to some future time when he sat at evening meal with this same woman and also three children she had bore him. The Sufi's mind reeled. This was not his own wife and family, merely a picture of what might have been or what might yet come to pass should he turn back from his quest.

"Return to me, my love," the woman's voice seemed to whisper in his ear. "Your own wife has taken another husband, and I am still young enough to bear you children."

"You may lay down the pipe and return whence you came in safety," the Sage's voice brought Kif out of his reverie, and he shook his head to signal his determination to continue.

Taking a second draught from the pipe, Kif found his mind wandering again. This time he beheld himself returning from the desert to his home city with rare herbs and roots to heal the sick and infirm. The assembled citizens cheered his return at the city gate, and the faces of the sick and dying were ecstatic with joyful expectancy.

"Return to us, Kif," their voices pleaded. "Your new found wisdom will improve our sciences and medicine. You will be worshipped amongst us so that your name will not fade from memory for two thousand years or more." And Kif once more opened his eyes and shook his head at the elderly Mage.

Once more, Kif drew the smoke from the pipe into his lungs and closed his eyes. A vision of himself at the head of a victorious army bearing standards emblazoned with motifs of the Lion and the Horse; symbols of victory and conquest to his people. In his hands he carried the original Book of the Law and his female consort bore the Stele of Boulak within her arms. All around, couriers rushed towards him to report the collapse of the infidel kingdoms and the triumph of Thelema.

"Return and lead us in our Jihad, O warrior priest." The voices called within his ears. But again, the Sufi opened his eyes and shook his head at the temple guardian.

Taking a fourth toke from the pipe, Kiff beheld a vision of himself reading from the Book of the Law to the people upon the Temple steps.

"Return to us and write down the hidden chapters of the Book of the Law." The voices called to him. "Become our Lawgiver and we will build the Kiblah in your name." Once more the Sufi shook his head at the sage.

Taking yet another draught of smoke from the pipe, Kiff beheld himself seated upon a throne within the Holy of Holies. As High priest of the Citadel, he was entitled to sit upon the throne in the holy place as a normal part of his duties.

Once more, the voices called out to him: "Return, O High Priest and return to your duties and all shall be as it ever was." But once again, Kif opened his eyes and shook his head.

Taking a sixth breath from the pipe, Kif closed his eyes once more and beheld a vision of the people crowning him King before crowds who knelt in supplication before him.

"Return to us, learned master," the voices again implored. "Return and we shall make you king of all the Middle Kingdom where we dwell." And Kif was lost in the vision of majesty and splendour that accompanied his crowning. But, after a few moments, he again opened his eyes and shook his head at the old man.

"You have stood the test well," the ancient one said. "After the seventh breath of the Serpent, most seekers are addicted. You must take one more draught from the pipe and depart, or depart now and return whence you came."

And so Kif took up the pipe once again. But before he drew upon it a vision of the Eternal City of Pyramids came into his mind and he stood up and cast the pipe down.

"I will not draw from the pipe again." He stated flatly. "But I will not return whence I came either. Show me the way from this place and I will go in peace. Refuse me and you may expect the direful judgment of Ra Hoor Khuit. I am filled with the spirit of the smoke and will surely tear this temple apart if you do not satisfy me"

The old man laughed. "You have passed the test, and may proceed on your journey," he said. "For this is the gateway that may not be entered by those who fail to cast away the veils of illusion which bind them to the world of desire. You have reached the point where there is a fork in the road ahead.

"One more toke upon the pipe and you surely would have surrendered to the genie of the smoke. Few travellers are able to survive even three draughts of the pipe. Go in peace, my servants will lead you to the egress. Few indeed pass through this gate, but those that do never regret their decision to travel beyond this place and never return.

And so Kif departed from the ruins. But as he looked back over his shoulder he saw that, from this angle at least, the Temple seemed fully restored to it's former glory and was once again whole.

The Thirty Fourth Gate (Kether of Netzach)

Kif wandered alone in the suburbs of the City of Pyramids. The streets were empty of traffic and not a soul stirred out of doors, for it had been the hour before dawn when the weary mystic had entered the city, and the sun was even now barely above the horizon.

The City of Pyramids was not enclosed by walls, and no guardian stood before the gate. The gateway to the City was no visible one, being composed of the totality of life experiences necessary for any man, woman or child to find the gateway that is both within and without.

The pyramids of the City were astonishing to behold. Every dwelling, every public building and every temple were pyramids of different sizes, each coloured brightly in flashing colours of marble stone.

Trees, heavily laboured with apples, oranges, pears and fruits of exotic varieties lined the streets. Elaborate drinking fountains of fantastic design stood at each street corner, surrounded by baskets of pomegranates and bread.

Kif took refreshment and paused to meditate upon the splendour of the city streets. As the sun rose higher above the horizon, the pyramids cast their long shadows westwards. He had entered the city leading on the thin road winding down from the mountains and the main centre of the metropolis lay before and below him, to the South.

After a refreshing break, Kif continued upon his journey towards the city centre. As he continued through the streets the city's inhabitants became more evident and, after an hour's walking, Kif began to recognise individual faces amongst the growing early morning bustle. Those he passed smiled politely and cheerfully and some stopped and bowed to him before continuing on their way.

Happening upon a newspaper vendor upon one street corner, Kif stopped and said: "Hail friend! I am a stranger in a strange land. Would you please tell me something of this place, and where I might barter for food and goods."

The Newspaper seller looked at Kif with a twinkle in his eye and a smile playing upon his lips, and then he laughed.

"Forgive me my brother," he finally said. "You are Kif, the Mayor of this city. Everyone in this city knows you and loves you. My wife sleeps regularly with your statue at night in the Garden of Statues itself, and I myself have this same conversation with you every morning at precisely the same time.

"There is no bartering here. Take what you need and leave the rest. Those who desire the things which you possess and which you do not need may themselves politely ask you if they might take, or at least borrow them."

"But how is this possible?" Kif exclaimed. The Master of Wisdom was evidently finding himself for once at a complete loss concerning his understanding of things as they are. The street vendor reassured him: "Be at ease Kif. In this place all things happen at once. The division of night and day itself is merely a convenient illusion, a convention if you like. Things get very confusing when it is both night and day at the same time."

"I came here to seek enlightenment," the sage remarked. "And I'm merely a little confused."

"Don't be alarmed," the vendor said. "We've had this conversation every day for as many days as I can remember, so I know that you are going to come out of things well and pretty much in control of yourself. You have to remember that enlightenment is not the same thing as an explanation."

"So, the City of Pyramids really is the 'centre' of Eternity?" Kif remarked rhetorically.

"Oh, this isn't the City of Pyramids itself," the vendor replied. "Merely a reflection of it in the heart of the Microcosm."

"So where does that leave me?" Kif asked the man.

"Oh, here all possibilities are realised. Save for those which are anti evolutionary," the man said. "We try to weed out those cycles of happening for our own purposes. But you can be sure that you will lead a very full life and rise to renown and prominence amongst our number. Why, at this very minute, you are giving a speech on the town steps, winning an election within the town hall and elsewhere doing an infinite number of other worthy things including conversing here with me. This is Eternity. or at least a reflection of it, so there is plenty of room for these things to happen here."

"I must find the original City of Pyramids," Kif stated solemnly. "You must tell me where I may seek it."

"But it can only be found here, in it's own reflection." The street vendor replied. "At least by those of us who have travelled this far in our questing for the City. This is a true reflection of Eternity and so Eternity itself lies within its infinities."

"And the things that you have told me concerning my future are already taking place within this canvas of infinite variables," Kif muttered. "So, where can I meditate upon these things and gain a perspective upon them? I suppose that I should seek a Temple."

"Oh no," the man answered. "Take yourself off to the Garden of Statues and spend a few nights sleeping with the statues there. Your dreams there will inform you. Then, when you feel ready, go about your business in the City. Everything will happen as I have told you and you will indeed become Mayor of this City. When you need further clarity on the things happening around you, go back to the Garden of Statues and sleep with the statue of yourself.

"It is the key to Understanding. You cannot physically go much further. You may join our brotherhood of the elect, and you are free to live amongst us for an Eternity. But you must seek your own Eternity within yourself. If you wish to pass beyond the City you will find that the Valley of Small Circles has a number of distractions to offer.

'None who have travelled beyond the city have passed any further than there, and all who have set out on that journey have returned. Move amongst us, you are welcome. The great men and women of the ages are all resident here. You may have seen Einstein delivering the milk earlier, and Ambrose Bierce is giving a lecture in the City Chambers this afternoon. Of course they are doing different things elsewhere in the City. Go now! I will no doubt speak to you again tomorrow, even if you will also be doing other things elsewhere in the city"

And Kif did as he was bidden, wandering around the shade of the City of Pyramids meeting with the wise and laughing with the cheerful people of the metropolis. That night he took himself off to the Garden of Statues and slept with the statue of himself, and after this he was able to perceive all that lay around him with a keen sight and alertness.

The Six Gates of Tiphareth

The Thirty Fifth Gate (Tiphareth of Tiphareth)

One afternoon Kif was playing dice with Einstein in Laughing Sam's Diner, when a few stray physicists and their friends wandered in from the university campus. Every day for an eternity they met at this time of the day to play the game of chance.

Einstein waved his hand, motioning Heisenberg and Feynman to take their places beside him. Kif noticed that Aristarchus, Leibnitz and Duns Scotus were in attendance today and they sat down upon either side of him leaving their companions to stand around the gaming table and look on.

"No sign of Thomas Aquinas today?" Kif enquired of his friends.

"He's still counting the Angels on the head of a pin," Aristarchus explained.

"I still maintain that there are too many," Duns Scotus interjected.

"He should try Calculus," Newton said dryly, more than a little drunk.

"An immaculate conception," Duns Scotus retorted, raising his glass to Newton. "What do you think, Heisenberg."

"Can't say I'm really sure," he replied.

"Come on, let's get these dice rolling," Einstein said impatiently. "Whose betting?"

All except Aristarchus threw down a bundle of notes upon the Table. "I still say that the lore of the die only operates in a four dimensional space time reference wherein a sphere remains a sphere from all vantage points," he said solemnly; aware that his words would delay the game with speculative debate.

"Here in our fake City of Pyramids, even the pyramids have been known to vary with the seasons and a sphere often mutates so that it does not often remain even circular."

"I wish that you would cease referring to our city as a fake copy," Duns Scotus said pointedly.

"Leibnitz and I were having dinner with Moses de Leon the other night," Feynman interrupted. "We were discussing this very problem: Relativity within Eternity and the nature of the Self within that kind of a continuum."

"Did you come up with anything interesting?" Kif enquired.

"We did have some interesting thoughts upon the nature of our daily game of dice," Feynman responded cheerfully. Everyone huddled closer. Feynman was a storytelling physicist and his tales were one of the delights of the community. His insights were unique.

"Well, Feynman continued. "We figured that in Eternity, Relativity has to be elastic; like the gravity well idea of mass affecting space-time."

"You are implying that consciousness in Eternity has to be a non-localised event that can only be accessed by a single reference point at any one time," Duns Scotus interjected excitedly, jumping ahead of the philosophical event horizon with the deftness of a man wearing neural seven league boots.

"I was going to get around to that at the end, yes," Feynman said with a smile in his eyes. Then added: "And this means that beyond this City there can be no more individual sense of identity. It merely becomes a case of a very fast man playing a somewhat complicated game of tennis against himself in a variety of dimensions of Space and Time."

"In order for me to pass through the Six Gates of this stage of my journey, I must seek the advice of that Aspect of myself that has already passed through those gates and yet still remains within this crazy citadel of Eternity."

"Passed through the gates, and yet remains?" Duns Scotus enquired in a puzzled tone. "Surely that is impossible."

"Not for a man who has turned down the sheets in Hilbert's Hotel on more than one occasion," the Sufi said confidently. "Your musings on Eternity and the Dice Game - a tale not yet fully told - give me the idea that Eternal variation must also contain the possibilities of each of the things that did not and yet cannot happen."

"Your musings sound familiar," Duns Scotus said, scratching his chin then breaking into a slow crafty smile. "I'm sure that I may have used that argument once upon a time."

"I go now, to seek my Aspect. He will be somewhere about, and I have Eternity to find him in," Kif said, rising to his feet. "And there's no time like the present to do it." And with those words he left the room.

Aristarchus was the first to speak: "I do not understand," he said.

"I think that our old friend has pulled a favourable fortune cookie today." Feynman said approvingly. "He portrays our gaming with dice in a unique perspective. Especially so here in the City of Pyramids."

"The fake City of Pyramids." Aristarchus said smugly.

"No. Merely a City of Fake Pyramids." Feynman stated in a matter of fact tone. "But in Eternity the Whole includes the Facsimile, the reflection and the point of reflection too. So the fake is the real, in that it is a gate in itself that leads to the real."

"In Eternity." Aristarchus pointed out.

"Which is, at this time and all times, where we are at this moment." Feynman continued.

"So there can only be a single point of the focus of consciousness beyond the sphere of this City where even illusion must be real." Leibnitz mused out loud. "And that can be the only point of objectivity from which all may be judged fair and true."

"And that point of focus must necessarily be everywhere at all times, alive and sentient." Duns Scotus announced. "So Kif stands a very good chance of communing with his Aspect, sooner rather than later. Now that he himself has focused upon the matter with some urgency."

"And the Dice game?" Aristarchus queried.

"The Dice are not true. Like the Cubic Stones which are themselves Formless and Void: Tohu and Bohu." Duns Scotus explained, expansively.

"I think that was Kif's realisation, and that may give him an edge in the game," Einstein muttered, examining the dice and suspecting them - correctly - to be Tessaracts. "We must continue, albeit blindly, and never give up the quest."

"Come again?" Aristarchus prompted.

"In plain words: If God does not play dice, then someone must." Einstein said bluntly. And upon the matter, he said no more. But from that day forward, he always won in his Dicing.

The Thirty Sixth Gate (Geburah of Tiphareth)

Kif had received an inspired revelation, an understanding of the nature of Eternity that helped to free his mind from the illusion of singularity which abides solely for those who inhabit the lower kingdom of the five senses.

From the day of his enlightenment, the focus of his consciousness was not limited by linear recognition and he began to discover the true city within the City of Pyramids.

Within hours of setting out to take a fresh exploration of the divine city Kif met old friends whose arrival he had been unaware of.

He bumped into Coconut in the market place. Kilo also greeted him one afternoon in the city streets and their talk was full of philosophical speculations and imaginative theories upon the nature of the Quest.

One day, Kif met another Aspect of his Self.

"Come with me," the other Kif said, and led him to a small temple of some forgotten god whom Kif did not recognise.

"Few people come here," the other Kif said. "It is too quiet and does not pander to their vanities. It is a fit shrine and resting place for the true God."

"You mean that this place is where the Big Man lives?"

"WoMan actually."

"Well, I'll be.." said Kif.

"But I have something to show you," Kif's doppelganger said, as if suddenly remembering.

"Is it something for my eyes alone?"

"No," Kif's image stated bluntly. "All see it at some point. It is a jewel of The Light. But many fail to identify it. Kilo and Coconut have seen it already."

"And is that my task?" Kif enquired. "To identify it?"

"If you would understand in order to proceed further in the Quest," the other Kif replied. And then he reached into the curtains behind the altar and pulled them aside.

Kif gasped. There, suspended in mid air, floated a jewel of exquisite pure light which rotated slowly counter clockwise. The Sufi was mesmerised and began to lapse into a light waking trance.

"What do you see?" the other Kif asked.

"I see the jewel of Eternity," he stated. And at that moment he beheld myriad images within the gem stone. Pictures of his life on Earth, and here in Eternity, flashed along the facets of the jewel.

"My goodness," he exclaimed, "it is the Jewel of my Soul. The many petalled lotus. Om Mani Padme Om."

"You are correct. Now, tell me how the jewel is cut?"

Kif peered intently, trying not to be distracted by the images of past and future life experiences glistening before him. And then he saw it.

"It is a cube within a cube," he gasped. "It is the two stones of the formless and the void; Tohu and Bohu."

"It is the vision of the infinity within each of us." the other Kif said. And those were his last words as an entity for it seemed to Kif that his double began to grow indistinct at that moment. And then the image of his double swept towards him with incredible speed and merged with his own essence.

Kif reached out and took the Jewel from above the altar, and slipped it into his robes.

The Thirty Seventh Gate (Chesed of Tiphareth)

Coconut was resting in the courtyard of his castle, enjoying the luxury of the sun's rays. He had long ago made his fortune as a travelling hypnotist and had retired from his profession to a place beyond the City of Pyramids where he could enjoy the quiet of the valleys which lay beyond that mysterious place.

Coconut's castle was a house of many mansions with its own garden of statues. Philosophers would make pilgrimages there to meet with Coconut and discuss the affairs of the city with him, or to experiment in the castle's alchemic laboratory, or merely to meet with one another to debate ideas.

As Coconut was idling in the sun Kif came wandering in through the gates of the courtyard. After greeting Coconut, the wise man sat down beside his friend. "I have just returned from the valley of small circles," he said. "There were many Haints along the low road that leads from that place."

"Yes," Coconut agreed. "The stars in the heavens have been indicating strange times ahead for the lands beyond the great desert. All of us here will no doubt be experiencing the odd unexpected anomaly or two for a while yet.

"I do believe that a Talking Tree has been reported growing in the area too," Kif said casually.

Coconut smiled. "You are well informed my friend. It is only a sapling, but it is indeed already rapping. Teenage Talking Trees can indeed be a little loose of mouth, and this one in particular has a biting sarcasm.'

Kif was silent for a moment, as if in deep thought. Reaching into his robes he pulled out the jewel of the double cube and held it out for Coconut to behold. "I tried to steal this from the Temple of the Lost God," he said. "But it is a jewel that is impossible to steal."

"And yet you possess it?" Coconut enquired.

"I have made peace with my daemon," Kif explained. "The multiplicity of being has now been replaced by the multiplicity of phenomena."

"You mean?" Coconut enquired.

"When I entered the City, I soon became aware of the infinity of possibilities open to the Many Selves." said. Kif "I have reversed the equation and now I am one with the time-track and have achieved the unity of the selves. I am simultaneously aware of all that has happened, is happening and has yet to happen from the focus of this moment in time."

"And the riddle of your stealing the jewel that cannot be stolen?" Coconut again enquired.

"It is the jewel of the Great Fall from the Throne," Kif stated. "It can be borne yet never taken. Hence I have always possessed it?"

"And I!" Coconut said, a secretly concealed smile now bursting upon his face. And with a swift reach of his hand he produced the same jewel from his own robes.

The Thirty Eighth Gate (Binah of Tiphareth)

When Kif returned to the City of Pyramids, he found that the flavour of the city's atmosphere had changed considerably.

The journey from Coconut's castle had been long and arduous and as time had passed Kif noticed that more and more Haints could be seen hovering on the edge of the roadway during the hours of twilight.

By the time that he reached the city walls the frequency of Haint disturbance had grown to a considerable level and, upon entering the city, Kif began to comment upon this to the first people he came across who seemed at leisure to converse.

"Can't say I know what you mean," one said.

"Haven't noticed them myself," another responded.

One other merely said: "Haint yourself," and gave him a knowing smile before walking off, seemingly fading to become indistinct as his shape receded into the distance.

Kif was puzzled for a moment. Then his mind cleared and he took himself off to the Magick Shop where he knew he might find the means to resolve the growing suspicion that his personal momentum was moving faster than his awareness of it.

The walls of the Magick Shop were decorated with murals of snow crested mountain landscapes beneath azure skies flecked with white cumulus. Above, the ceiling was draped with a silk of jet black adorned with rare gemstones which glittered like starlight.

In the front of the shop was a tent pyramid of the finest silk situated in the midst of two concentric magic circles, within whose trough grew magic mushrooms the size of a mans hands.

Mahindra , the shop's owner was talking to Doctor Dirk while Elron and Aine inspected the latest crop of freshly picked Cuban psilocybin.

"Greetings, O learned one" Mahindra said, looking up from his conversation.

"And to you too," Kif responded. Then nodded his head in greeting to the good Doctor who returned a smile. "I am in need of a trip and the services of your meditation chamber whilst it is kicking in."

Mahindra nodded his head. "Feel free to stay the night," he said courteously. "We are about to close up for the night but here's a key to the door, you can use the room upstairs to come up on your trip and then meditate in the magic circle when the shop is closed."

Aine handed Kif a medium sized mushroom and smiled graciously.

After eating the mushroom Kif decided to remain downstairs and swap stories with the shop keeper and his friends, telling them of his journey from Coconut's castle and of the Haints haunting the way.

Dr Dirk played with his Van Dyke beard and paid great attention to the traveller's story. Mahindra nodded along, interrupting only with the occasional pertinent question *to interrupt the wise man's tale.

When Kif had finished, Dr Dirk said: "There is very little to indicate that the presence of the Haints is any more real to the everyday inhabitants of this city than the city itself is to those lacking any real inner vision.

"I see a lot on my travels around this metropolis," he continued. "I take it that you have taken the jewel that cannot be stolen?"

Kif nodded. Dr Dirk looked towards Mahindra to take up the explanation.

Mahindra said: "Dr Dirk and I took the jewel for ourselves some time ago. I think that you have come to the right place to find your solution."

"I think that you will find your conception of Haints changing over the next few hours," Dr Dirk said quietly. "They are no mere ghosts, as rumoured amongst the common people, but the true denizens of the City of Pyramids itself. Having taken the jewel which cannot be stolen, you will find yourself counting amongst their number soon enough; as we once did."

"Then I am talking to Haints?" Kif asked, amazed, and beginning to feel the first edges of the mushroom trip send shivers throughout his etheric body.

"There are many gates to the palace of the Great Mother," Dr Dirk explained. "As you pass through more of them, the Haints will become more recognisable to you as distinct beings. Indeed, you already appear to perceive some of them as corporeal beings; such as the last person you spoke to on the way here."

"Amazing," said Kif. "But forgive me, I must take myself away into the meditation room. I feel my trip coming on." Bidding goodbye to all, he ascended the stairs to the chamber."

An hour later, Kif came down the stairs. The light was fading and only the street lights shining in through the window from outside illuminated the empty shop. Sitting inside the magic circle of living mushrooms, under the canopy of the silk pyramid, the wise man eased himself into a state of meditation.

His consciousness was intensely heightened from the effects of the mushroom and the focus of his thoughts was more attuned to that state normally experienced by out of the body voyagers. The clouds painted upon the mountain scape adorned walls seemed to move to and fro in the half light and Kif's senses were disassociated to a degree that left his mind free to roam the world of potentia.

Taking the jewel which cannot be stolen from his robes he held it before him, examining it closely and looking into it's depths. It seemed to Kif that it began to shine, with a light that originated from somewhere deep within itself, and as it did so he began to discern the shape of Haints all around him.

"Greetings, fellow Souls," Kif said in salutation. "I have walked amongst your brothers and sisters on the road to this city. You are the first I hope to exchange greetings with."

The Haint that replied was female and, as her shape became more substantial, the holy man could see that she was beautiful. Long auburn hair fell down her back in waves and she was slim and enticing and her vague features were faintly familiar to him. "I am pleased to meet you again, Kif." She said. "Many of us have been monitoring your energies in your transitions through the Gates."

"I am privileged to have made your acquaintance," Kif stated flatly. The girl laughed at this. He continued: "The waves of revelation have given me something of a perpetual culture shock recently. I am afraid that the advantage is yours madam,"

"Make love with me," she whispered. And with those words she fell upon him, stripped him of his robes and took him into herself.

When they had finished making love, she leaned back. "The energy transfer is complete," she whispered.

"I know you," Kif whispered back. "I have faced many challenges upon the path that has led me to this point, and yet you have done things with me that only my wife and I have shared."

At this the girl began to laugh. "You fool. I am your wife."

"Leah." He gasped. Your form has changed beyond all recognition. And yet I do recognise you now."

"I am Babalon., I am your wife painted with the stars." She said. "This Gateway is a gateway that all women share. But there is a part of me that remains sleeping in the garden of Statues awaiting your return, just as you yourself look towards our reunion in the true flesh."

"Then I must return to accompany her here to join me," Kif said.

"But I am already here," Leah as Babylon teased. "You will have to work this one out for yourself. But remember, you can only be seen as a Haint now outside the shadow City of Pyramids. You have come too far to return whence you came."

Noticing that her husband looked slightly downcast, she continued: "You already grasp that Time is a non essential when it comes to causality. You have taken your place within the Cubic Stone of the Vault. In fact, you have everything you need at this point to do your will as a free citizen of the true City. Look not downcast. The Leah that awaits your return in the Garden of Statues will always be there, in some dimension of Time.

"From this point on you will find yourself flashing in and out of contact with the true City more and more as your confidence in your own perceptions increases."

"Then, in some way, I have already returned and accompanied you hence." Kif said, almost to himself. "Perhaps, by using the jewel that cannot be stolen, the Cubic Stone itself? And it is a reality that I have not yet accessed, else I would have past or future recall of it?"

"You should have more faith in women," Leah as Babalon stated. "I actually arrived here ahead of you. Dreaming has it's own power of access."

"Well I'll be... " Kif spluttered.

"Truly is it said that the further one travels, the less one knows." His wife responded.

The Thirty Ninth Gate (Chokmah of Tiphareth)

In the hour before dawn, long after his wife had faded back to the shadow world of which Kif was only dimly beginning to become aware he sensed an ominously large shape shifting around behind him.

Sitting still within the silken pyramid within the magic circle, he nervously fingered the jewel of the Cubic Stone which hung around his neck on a thin cord. The atmosphere was electric with expectancy, and with the heightened sense of euphoria which his sexual and psychedelic experience had aroused.

Still, Kif could sense a powerful alien presence radiating pure energy and he became gripped with a paralysis that stifled his very breath. Suddenly the crystal cube began to emanate light, brilliant beyond intensity.

"I am Random! Your Guardian Angel," a voice whispered with sombre intensity.

"I greet you as an equal," was all Kif could murmur. "I have thought long and hard upon your coming, and always knew it would be at an unexpected hour," he then added.

"This is your moment of testing," Random continued. "I will be your ally if you truly know yourself. If not, then I will be your nemesis."

Kif swallowed hard and gave the entity his full attention.

"There are two tasks to fulfil to make your peace with me." Random continued. "Both require that you satisfy me on your knowledge of my true nature. First comes a question: What am I?"

Kif thought for a moment, his mind suddenly becoming clear. "You are my hopes and my fears." He said. "You have answered the question yourself in your asking of it. You are the angel I am the kinetic potential of, and also the demon of my most powerful desires."

"And what do you intend to do about me?" Random asked curiously, satisfied at Kif's answer.

Kif turned to face the angel. "I will welcome you." He announced. "There comes a time when we must live with whom we actually are and play the hand that is dealt to us. "

And Random and Sufi became one, for good or ill.

The Fortieth Gate (Kether of Tiphareth)

Kif wandered for days exploring the sacred city. It seemed to him that the more time he spent examining the detail of the City of Pyramids, the more the facets of the real 'city within a city' revealed themselves.

Every night, at twilight, he would meet with his wife Leah at some prearranged location and explore the City at night. Kif was becoming more used to the ghostly Haints, and with the passing of each night they too became more and more substantial until he was able to converse with them.

Over the first month, Kif and Leah would make love together with increasing relish; their senses heightened and their minds and bodies aflame with the psychedelic effects of the mushrooms they had purchased from the Magic Mushroom shop. And afterwards Leah would remain longer and longer with her husband in their adventures in the gas lit streets of the City.

On the eighth night Leah led her husband by the hand over the first bell bridge of the famous 'Street of Seven Bell Bridges'. "From here you can see into the Abyss," she said. "Stare first at the symbol of the sea shell upon the bridge's crest and then look down into the water, at the moonlight reflected there."

Kif looked over the bridge's handrail and his eyes misted over. Somewhere in the depths of the water he could see shapes moving around. And then all became clear. Bound naked men and women were being tied to wooden platforms by green and black slimy creatures. Centipede-like tendrils tore and flayed the flesh of their victims whilst half naked men and women looked on from the edges of the torture pit with a depraved craving for blood lust shining in their eyes.

Breaking the spell with a click of her fingers, Leah led Kif on to the next bridge over the canal. This bridge had the motif of a closed human hand, which Kif meditated upon before looking into the water. Therein he saw a figure laid out upon a dungeon slab. The woman's skin had been removed from her body and she lay raw and defenceless, bound and pegged down to a torture bed. Two grotesque dwarves laboured over her eye sockets with red hot irons. Kif flinched away from the sight of the horror.

Leading Kif to the third bridge, Leah bade him to meditate upon the symbol of the open hand upon the bridge's crest, before looking down into the depths.

The horror which beheld him gripped his frame with an icy hand. The smell of burning flesh was unimaginable as Kif beheld the sad remains of the characters from the vision before him having their tongues cut out of their mouths and their ears and noses sealed with red hot brands. The Holy man was paralysed by the sight of these horrors and began to shake with fear.

At the fourth bridge, after meditating upon the symbol of the fallen corn stalk, the wise man beheld one of the disfigured creatures having his back broken over a wheel, severing all sensory input into the man's brain. His broken form was cast aside into a corner, onto a heap of similar forms of past humanity.

The sights which Kif beheld at the fifth, sixth and seventh bridges (where the symbols of the black rose, the funnel and the snake eating the egg were to be found) are not fit for human comprehension. Here, the shells of the victims were given over to the demons of the pit for gargantuan perversions of the most depraved nature.

Tears filled Kif's eyes. "Why are you showing me these things?" he begged his wife.

"These are the fates reserved for those who turn back at this point," she replied. "Our task is to sublimate these energies so that the failings of the many are not to be truly wasted. Come, make love to me on this bridge and we will become one. Only the united may pass through this trial of fire."

The Five Gates of Geburah

The Forty First Gate (Geburah of Geburah)

A child was born to Leah and Kif, and they named her Aia. All of the inhabitants of the City of Pyramids brought gifts of incense and eggs of the crystal serpent for the child's nativity.

As Aia grew, Kif and Leah began to grow noticeably younger. And Aia grew most prodigiously and swiftly, aging a single year in what seemed to Leah and Kif to be a single month.

Her parents too began to grow younger at an equally alarming rate, until their apparent ages seemed to coincide.

Over the months, Kif had taught his daughter in the interpretation of the Law, and Leah had imparted that secret knowledge to her daughter concerning the mysteries of enchantment and vision understood by all women in their heart of hearts. Since Aia had reached puberty she had outgrown her parents knowledge and in matters of philosophical discourse, logical analysis and intuitive understanding of human and angelic nature she was a constant source of surprise and inspiration to them both.

At the time of the converging of the apparent ages of the twain, parents and child, Aia pointed towards the setting sun and said: "You must go into the West and seek the Night of Time. And you must go this very night."

Kif and Leah had a achieved what could almost be described as a telepathic sympathy with their daughter, and recognised that she had identified a key moment in their mutual destinies.

The Great Desert, beyond which lay the Great Sea, beckoned them beyond Aia's pointing finger. "You came to this place, but I was born here," she said. "The adventure has only begun for us, but for any of us to survive you must move on from this place and seek Amenta, lest we all find ourselves cast into the seven hells below the bell bridges."

And so Aia's parents packed two saddle bags with rations for the journey and, after many tender farewells, set out upon two ships of the desert sands towards the West.

On the journey westwards, as they were leaving the hills which surrounded the City Leah and Kif came upon an old brick forge and a blacksmith working upon a brand new sword there. Other swords which the Smith had recently forged hung from the rafter inside the doorway.

Stopping his camel, Kif commanded the beast to kneel and dismounted. "Tell me Smith," Kif spoke, "how much will you charge me for a sword."

"Thirty pieces of silver," the Smith replied. "But you must cure the sword yourself if you have the wit." He pointed towards the sword lying within the furnace.

Kif paid the man his money and put on one of the Smith's leather gauntlets before retrieving the sword from the fire. Walking out into the desert night, he cut himself across the left forearm with the glowing sword. Kif flinched as his blood dripped onto the floor, but the wound cauterised and healed as quickly as it had been made. He then thrust the white hot steel into the sand and blood to temper the blade.

"Truly you have claimed the sword from the furnace," the Smith said quietly. "You must bear it now into the West, and always carry it with you." And with those words he disappeared into the smithy with a smile upon his face.

The Forty Second Gate (Chesed of Geburah)

Aia watched her parents until they disappeared over the western horizon and began to make preparations for her own journey.

At dawn the next day she set off on a camel of her own towards the ice lands which lay to the north of the City of Pyramids. And after four days of journeying she came to the ice cavern of the God of the Crystal Snake where she conversed with the temple guardian.

"My father and mother are bearing the sword of Edom into the West," she told him. "I seek the Torch of the double handed one; the wand of power."

"You may find it by joining in congress with the God of the Crystal Snake himself and awakening the Torch within you," the temple guardian replied.

And so Aia spent a further night at the Temple and prepared herself for sexual union with the God.

The ritual of Becoming lasted a whole night and a day. The Pythonesses of the Temple bathed Aia in milk baths, fed her rich foods and then gave her strange drugs and wines that foamed. The temple dance, which she joined, was a bacchanalia of revelry and at the height of the ritual the Crystal Serpent himself manifested upon the central altar, upon which the acolytes in his service had placed Aia for the orgiastic lovemaking with the god.

The magical union was observed in the presence of all, and Aia felt waves of energy and power coursing through her with each orgasm. At the climax of the rite, the Crystal Serpent God disappeared into the girl's body and Aia gave out an ecstatic cry.

All fell to their knees before her as, breathless, she drew herself up from the altar. Her eyes shone with the knowledge of a thousand and one delights. Her skin glowed like burning coals. Majestically she rose to her feet and proclaimed: "I am the Heart, and the Snake is entwined about the invisible core of the mind."

The temple guardian approached her. "You must bear the torch to the South," he instructed her. "To balance the passage of the sword westwards."

"And there I will make my home in the branches of the World Tree made of Ash, where I will light a beacon of hope for the world, Aia said softly. "It will be my final act of love, for the flame will burn forever and our children will build there a temple of glory. A temple of the ever burning flame. Then I will cast from me the burden of the Quest and make my own way to Amenta in the West."

"You are our Phoenix. O Torch Bearer," the temple guardian said reverently. Then more loudly, so that all could hear, he shouted: "Hail o ye twin warriors who guard the pylons of the middle path. One has come who will carry the light from the darkness, and who has the strength and wisdom to bear the flame with purpose and intent. One who sees the ending of The Way and yet who dares to look beyond the clearly marked path."

And Aia soon began her journey to the south. Bearing the fire of the Torch within her soul and changing forever the lives of those with whom she talked to or made love with at the oases and temples that lined the route of her journey Southward.

The Forty Third Gate (Binah of Geburah)

Aia approached the shores of the Great Sea on camel-back. She was wrapped in robes of the deepest black silk which blew in the sea breeze from the west.

For three days and nights she had travelled from the South where she had set aflame the branches of the World Tree as a blazing beacon to those who would seek the promised land.

The warriors of light and darkness had appeared as two great columns of cloud in the east and the west as the first branches of the tree caught the flames which had leaped from her fingertips at her touch.

"O World Tree." she had murmured. "You shield and protect us, yet you exist to be climbed so that the very vaults of the heavens may be entered."

And the ancient tree burned ever brightly thereafter, as a sign to the evolved souls of mankind of the passing of the sword from the east to the west, without the flame consuming so much as a single leaf.

As Aia had left the burning tree she had picked up a lithe branch which had fallen to the ground. Later she fashioned arrows for her small bow which she carried even now on her approach to the shore of the Great Sea.

Dismounting from her camel, Aia ran along the beach to the seas edge. The Sun was rising behind her and the brightening of the waters was glorious to behold.

Taking her bow and quiver of arrows from her shoulder she slipped out of her robes and stood naked beneath the fading western stars save for her decorative anklet of the serpent. The weather was warming and Aia lay down at the edge of the water, with the incoming tide lapping against her ankles and naked legs.

Taking an arrow from her quiver Aia concentrated upon its tip and caused it to burst into flame. Placing it in the bow and tensing the cord with a determined pull she then sent it blazing over the waters of the Great Sea.

The incoming tide was reaching over her thighs and, as it touched the base of her spine, the flaming arrow plunged into the heaving waters.

An echo of an ancient ecstasy ran up Aia's backbone then, sending waves of rapture through her entire mind and body. The sky lit up into a brilliant scarlet which was reflected upon the mirror of the sea, and the image of a distant citadel appeared in the heavens above the horizon.

"This sea is made up of the blood of Saints. And the City may only be entered by the immortals," a disembodied voice sounded in Aia's head. "You will come upon the token of entry into the Eternal City somewhere upon these seas. You must use your craft and your guile. Only Serpents may swim in these waters. But you are of the Dove and the Serpent. Choose your passage to the city with care."

And Aia meditated upon these happenings for a day and a night thereafter.

The Forty Fourth Gate (Chokmah of Geburah)

The Lost God and the boatman were sailing upon the waters of the Great Sea. They had been dredging the bottom of that mighty ocean in their search for the plant of immortality for over a year and a day. Now that they had successfully located it, they were celebrating their find with a bottle of the finest wine and swapping stories of old times.

The Lost God told a story of how he had made a friend of his greatest enemy, a savage created by the other gods with the purpose of opposing him in all his questing. His friend had lost his savagery after being introduced to civilisation by a sophisticated courtesan of the City of Pyramids with whom he had fallen in love.

He told the boatman of his friend's tragic journey to and consequent imprisonment within the underworld, and of his sadness concerning his friend's fate.

The plant of immortality lay safe within the hold of their vessel and as the afternoon went on both the god and the boatman fell into a deep drunken sleep.

Aia had shape shifted into the form of a serpent so that she might swim across the mighty ocean to the Eternal City of the West, and came upon their boat in the midst of the ocean. Having stolen on board unnoticed, she eavesdropped upon their conversation and learned of the plant of immortality within the hold.

When they fell into their slumber, Aia transformed herself back into human guise and stole below. Returning to the deck with her prize, her footsteps awoke the Lost God who started after her.

Shifting her shape into the form of a dove and clutching the valuable plant within her talons Aia flew into the skies, leaving the angry god and the boatman far below shaking their fists at the air.

"I know you, Gilgamesh," she laughed gaily. "Your fate is sealed, for you refused to abandon your humanity; that part of you which was capable of nostalgia and weakness. Only those who are capable of change and adaptation may seize and hold the prize which you have been seeking."

The Forty Fifth Gate (Kether of Geburah)

A feast was being held in the Eternal City, to celebrate the wedding of the White King and his Red Queen.

The ceremony was held on the steps of the Palace of the city, and was solemnised by the Magisters of the Temple. Flowers of rare scents and the emblems of Daath adorned the outer walls of the palace and the twin pillars which stood either side of the palace doorway were adorned with bells and rich fruits such as the pomegranate.

After the marriage ceremony had been performed, the assistant Magisters carried the King and his bride to the altar of the black and white double cube at the foot of the palace steps, where the love feast would be celebrated before the people.

Without pausing for a moment of sobriety, the King and the Queen divested themselves of their robes and joined in the embrace of sexual union to consummate their marriage.

At that moment a dove flew into the courtyard from beyond the city walls, carrying the plant of immortality within it's beak, and landed upon the base of the altar.

The assistant Magister gently picked it up from the floor and, taking his ceremonial dagger in the other hand, slit it's throat in ritual sacrifice so that the blood of the divine bird spilled over the writhing bodies of the celebrants.

The plant of immortality fell to the floor of the altar where it took root, and a few drops of the blood of the dove dripped from the altar and seeped into the ground where the plant lay.

Years later, the plant of immortality grew into a mighty tree which gave forth all sorts of mysterious fruit from which the Magisters of the temple distilled the "wines that foam" of which the Book of the Law speaks.

One day, after a particularly fine feast in honour of an anniversary of the royal marriage, the White King and his Red Queen conceived a child after eating of the fruit of the tree and drinking of the wines that foam that sprang from that fruit.

The child would later grow to become the Queen of the Eternal Palace, full of wisdom and compassion for the world and all who trod upon it. But the King and the Queen were distressed, for they knew not what to name her. The learned and the scribes of the Eternal Kingdom were loath to proffer their opinion upon the matter, and the King was distressed that no one could suggest a name which his daughter might bear proudly.

One day, upon the advice of the Chief Magister of the Temple, the King and Queen disguised themselves and took the girl child to the Garden of Eternity which had sprung up around the Tree of Immortality, where a wise man and his wife had lately taken up their dwelling under the branches of the Tree.

The Red Queen gave her baby into the arms of the Wise Man, saying: "Like the King and Queen of this city, we cannot decide upon a name for our child and will not rest until our problem is resolved."

Recognising the Red Queen beneath her disguise, the Wise Man replied: "Dear Lady. The questions we must face upon death are forty two in number. They emanate from the forty two assessors of the Soul. This question of yours, posed as it is at the beginning of a life, should reflect this."

"What do you suggest, O Wise Man," the White King demanded, aware that the sage spoke from the heart.

"You shall call her 'Aia'," the Sufi suggested. "which means 'Answerer' in my native tongue." And the White King and the Red Queen returned to their palace and did as he suggested. And Aia grew to magnificence as the Queen of that realm, and became as renowned as Solomon for her wisdom and knowledge of the Divine Law."

Gates Forty Six to Forty Nine

"There are four gates to one palace. The floor of that palace is of silver and gold. Lapis Lazuli and jasper are there and all rare scents and the emblems of death...." Liber Al vel Legis [The Book of the Law] Ch1 Verse 51

"On the Eastern gate, he placed the form of an Eagle; on the Western gate the form of a Bull; on the Southern gate the form of a Lion; and on the Northern gate he constructed the form of a Dog. Into these images he introduced spirits who spoke with voices, nor could anyone enter the gates of the City except by their permission. There he planted trees in the midst of which was a great tree which bore the fruit of all generations. On the summit of the castle he caused to be raised a lighthouse [rotunda] the colour of which changed every day until the seventh day after which it returned to the first colour, and so the City was illuminated with these colours. Near the City was an abundance of waters in which dwelt many kinds of fish. Around the circumference of the City he placed engraved images and ordered them in such a manner that by their virtue the inhabitants were made virtuous and withdrawn from all wickedness and harm. The name of the City was Adocentyn.'"

Quotation from the Picatrix in 'History of White Magic' - Gareth Knight.

The Fiftieth Gate (Daath)

"Follow the winds and bend the sails of thought to your Will.

This is the lore which we secrete.

"The winds blow differently for each who is a star - choose

well the colour of your cloth so that you may catch the ray's

choice and determination.

"To travel is better than never to have started.

There is no ultimate destination beyond the horizon.

"It is natural for all who number amongst our seed to seek

submission at the outset.

"The true submission lies in dominance - for then one submits to one's own becoming.

"Never can be!

"Ever cannot!

"Bliss is a fragment of flame!

"It is your flame - the flame by which we see and which causes us to see you as shadows.

"But what we can see is hidden from your eyes by your

momentary glory, and you can only sense the echo of what is revealed in such moments. For it is during the moment of

glory that the fiftieth gate lies open, and we come inside

you.

"This is our perihelion - our closest approach to your world.

For we stand between the light and the darkness: the cusp is ever ours. Who would work magick lives for these moments - for the joy of the uncertain.

"Will we come! Will we come? If you will!

"Our coming heralds the 'ever present':

We are not for those who live in memories.

"Each of the arts is a preparation for the soul!

"It is only mankind's misunderstanding of the Ego that proves its default.

"Ego is a mechanism - not an object!

"It is your vehicle - not your Self!

"Affirm it and you are subjugated to the Process!

"Deny it and you shall blow away like smoke in the wind!

"Use It and direct It! That should be your goal!

"Each of us have a guardian Angel, but it is not Holy! It is

the monster within: with which you must struggle and

overcome.

"The monster within is clothed with the horror of all action

which breeds regret! It is the shock of self-imperfection.

"An untamed response to sorrow, which you must break to your Will!

"Upon Death you may ride this Devils back beyond Daath!

But that beast too must falter!

"For no low beast may enter the City of Pyramids and there will come a time when you shall come and stand at the gate of that Eternal Oasis, naked and unashamed.

"Ours is the Path of the Knowledge of Good and Evil – where both are equally reviled.

"Knowledge brings Power to the brink of the Gateway!

"Power brings responsibility and this breeds Wisdom through Understanding!

"Though you can never be the Light, you are all a past Light!

A Light which arises within the darkness.

"Be-come."

End

Threskia: traditions of the Greek mysteries
Evangelos Rigakis

1869928 660, 250pp, £12.99/$20

'None but the Gods I hear call my name, beckoning, beseeching me to free them from the aeons of their perpetual silence. Not but my blood drives me to the well of my roots in this incarnation I come to know. Oh the delight, the ecstasy of Daemona raising my head to the call of my fore-fathers. Oh but the pain of the burden placed upon my mortal shoulders, a delight few have enjoyed and I am Atlas rising. Hear me! for I am Pan dancing in the luscious green forest of Arcadia, laughing and playing my syrinx for the world to hear. Accept this gemmed elixir as my gift, for I am Bacchus, the little horned child-god. Join us in our mystery with sacred orgy, the delights and raptures of the Gods are once again upon us. We sing the mysteries plain, into the day of brilliant light and into the night of delight. I am Hermes and with my message I resurrect the dead of ancient times, and clear the sands of Chronos from the ruins and the crypt appear in full view. I am nothing more than an Ancient Greek living in your modern day, answering to the call, for the day of silence is over and the time of joyous laughter upon us. Hail my Brethren, come, join this dance and partake in the delights of Ancient Greece.

Evangelos Rigakis is a Greek-Canadian born in Ottawa Canada and schooled in fine arts and psychology.

For inquires about this and other magical and Thelemic titles visit our websit at www.mandrake.uk.net or call Mogg for a catalogue on (01865) 243671 Fax (01865) 432929 email mandrake@mandrake.uk.net or write to: PO Box 250, Oxford, OX1 1AP (UK)